everyday miracles

NOELLE NELSON, Ph.D.

PRENTICE HALL PRESS

Library of Congress Cataloging-in-Publication Data

Nelson, Noelle C.
    Everyday miracles : transforming your life using what you already have /
Noelle Nelson.
        p.   cm.
    ISBN 0-7352-0159-5 (pbk.)
    1. Conduct of life.   I. Title.
BF637.C5 N45 2000
158—dc21

99-088621
CIP

Acquisitions Editor: *Susan McDermott*

Production Editor: *Jacqueline Roulette*

Formatting/Interior Design: *Robyn Beckerman*

Printed in the United States of America

    10 9 8 7 6 5 4 3 2 1

ISBN 0-7352-0159-5

PRENTICE HALL PRESS
Paramus, NJ 07652

On the World Wide Web at http://www.phdirect.com

*This book is dedicated to my clients,
who have taught me what courage really is,
and what a grand adventure life can truly be.
Thank you.*

Acknowledgments

It's always a miracle to me when what starts out as a mere idea—something ephemeral, often hard to pin down—turns into a manuscript and then becomes a book—something truly solid and concrete. That miracle never happens without the contribution of many people, the first of whom is my editor, Susan McDermott. Once again, Susan has been marvelously supportive, encouraging, and patient throughout, for which I am deeply grateful. I am also thankful to Prentice Hall for believing in *Everyday Miracles* and publishing it. My thanks to Jacqueline Roulette for her terrific copy editor's eye, which has saved me from embarrassing "bloopers" that seem to crop up despite my best efforts. I also appreciate the efforts of Prentice Hall's fine publicity department, headed by Yvette Romero. My everlasting gratitude goes to Diane Rumbaugh, for her unceasing efforts on my behalf, her constant good humor, steadfastness, and patience. Finally, my heartfelt thanks to my family and friends, without whom there would be far fewer miracles in my life!

Contents

Contents

Contents

Contents

Introduction

Life is a gift. It is precious and wonderful and meant to be lived in joy and celebration. Deep down, we all know that. It just doesn't seem that way when you've had a lousy day at work (your boss insisting you cram 10 hours of work into 8); your partner is in a foul mood and taking it out on you (or you can't find a partner to be grumpy with you in the first place); your transmission is making that weird noise again, which the mechanic swears he fixed and charged you a fortune for; you're practically living on antacid tablets; you can't lose those ten pounds you promised yourself you'd shed before summer, and your slim, trim so-athletic-I-could-kill-them friend keeps saying "But it's so easy, just jog five miles a day," as if that'll ever happen; you're worried sick your job is going to disappear or you'll lose that promotion to someone ten years younger/older; you've just spent two sweaty hours inching your way through gridlocked traffic; the dog threw up on the carpet (again); the kids are out of control, yelling and screaming at each other (or you wish you had kids to yell at each other); you're out of milk, cat food, *and* dental floss; and the only thing in the mailbox is more bills you can't keep up with. And this is just an ordinary day. . . .

That's when you scream, cry, or mutter through gritted teeth, "I need a miracle!" And so you do. More than that, you *deserve* a miracle. The good news is that miracles are something you can have, miracles not only of divine intervention, but miracles of your own design.

For what is a miracle? An answer to your prayers, a wish fulfilled, a dream realized. For most of us, the miracles we seek aren't the raising of the dead or the parting of the Red Sea. Mostly we yearn for everyday miracles, positive and gratifying solutions to the challenges of our everyday lives, help with the things that go wrong in the ordinary course of living: the frustrations, disappointments, aggravations, missed opportunities, betrayals, and the sheer exhaustion of struggle and effort. These are the miracles that make life so much easier, so much more rewarding and satisfying. These are the miracles you can create for yourself in your life. These are the miracles this book can help you bring to pass.

But how? What does it take to make a miracle? Miracles are not something you beat, yank, or manipulate out of the universe. Miracles are something you invite into your life so that they can come to you in their own way.

Miracles don't happen by just opening your mouth and saying "I want . . ." Miracles happen by knowing how to set things up, how to create the conditions that make it possible for miracles, positive win-win solutions to your problems of everyday living, to flow into your life. *Everyday Miracles* shows you, through practical examples and vignettes, specifically how to create the conditions to let miracles flow. In *Everyday Miracles,* you will find powerful insights, skills, and tools to help you create miracles in your day-to-day life.

Each of the topics in *Everyday Miracles* speaks to one of life's challenges, be that in the arena of family, work, relationships of all types, or self-growth and empowerment. To get the most out of *Everyday Miracles,* first read through the whole book. Then work with the insights and information at your own pace. Some of the miracle-making skills will apply to your life situation immediately. Great! Some of the chapters will seem less relevant to your life right now. No problem. Think of *Everyday Miracles* as your miracle-making resource. Whenever you are having difficulty in a certain area of your life, just go back to *Everyday Miracles* and zero in on the topic that seems to apply best. *Everyday Miracles* can give you miracle-making skills, the information and awareness necessary to help you create a rich and rewarding life day by day.

Life is a gift. Live it the way it was meant to be lived—as a joyous, successful, love-filled adventure, with its ups and downs, yes, but overall, happy! Let *Everyday Miracles* help you create miracles of joy and success in your everyday life, miracles that make life sweet and worth living. Welcome to a life where your every day is filled—with miracles!

Dear Readers: I value your thoughts and comments, and can be reached via E-mail at nnelson@www.dr.noellenelson.com or Voicemail at (310) 859-4604.

Noelle Nelson

The Impossibility of Failure

Babies have a wonderful gift for success. Before a certain age, we tackle all our goals with utter delight, great energy, and unstoppable enthusiasm. Watch a baby learning to feed itself: the baby grabs the utensil wherever she can—middle, end, it doesn't matter—PLOW! into the mashed carrots the spoon goes, splattering carrots all over the walls, the baby, Mom, so what? The baby doesn't care; all the baby knows is WOW! sheer joy—"How about that, I got the spoon in!" Next step: Find the mouth; this can take a bunch of tries, but does the baby carefully plot out where the spoon should go? No, the baby pretty much shoves the spoon anywhere in the general vicinity of her face, and somewhere along the line some of the carrots actually come in contact with the mouth. ZOOWIE! The baby shrieks with ecstatic abandon—SUCCESS!!!

Notice that nowhere along this adventuresome path does the baby stop and say: "Hey, kid, you're not getting this fast enough, it took you 17 tries to find your mouth, little Janie down the street did it in 12." Nor does the baby stop at try #14 and say: "I give up, I'll never get this, I'm a loser, it's all downhill from here." No. The baby has no concept of failure, neither in terms of the goal (feeding herself), nor in terms of herself as being able/unable to meet the challenge.

What the baby does have is something tremendously important that we all would do well to remember: a completely positive attitude toward her efforts, and committed focus. Let's take a look at each of these.

1. *A completely positive attitude.* Babies do not beat on themselves; that's a talent we acquire later. You don't see a baby stop, spoon in midliftoff, saying "Rats, I should have done that better, I'm just such a stupid, slow learner." The baby lifts the spoon, smacks herself a load of carrots on the nose, and simply goes: "Woops! Wrong hole—no sweat, let's do it again!"

Consistently reward yourself for your efforts, evaluate what didn't work purely in terms of how you can get closer to your goal on the next try, and go for it. Soon enough, you'll find your mouth.

2. *Committed focus.* Committed focus is when you choose your goal (focus), and then are 100 percent committed to achieving that goal. When you are 100 percent committed to achieving your goal, you cannot fail, you can only succeed to varying degrees. The baby may not feed herself brilliantly, but she feeds herself. For example, if you want to learn computers (focus), commit yourself 100 percent to that task, and you will learn computers. You may never be particularly fast at it, you may never invent any groundbreaking software, but you will know how to operate a computer. Your success is restricted only by the limits of your creativity, and if you stop and think about it, that's hardly a limitation at all.

You cannot fail. It is utterly impossible, given committed focus, to fail. You may have a more limited success than you desire, but you cannot fail. So grab your spoon and go for it—success is so much fun!

W*hat would you attempt to do if you knew you could not fail?*

DR. ROBERT SCHULLER

Transforming Parent into Adult

Whether you're 22 or 52, most of us have a parent or two still around. Have you noticed how difficult it is for parents to stop parenting? Parenting is such a huge and arduous and weighty responsibility that once parents have gotten the hang of it, they seem to want to keep doing it forever. The problem is that if you're a 26-year-old trying to figure out who you are and how you want to be in the world, having a permanent parent telling you how to do it, or more commonly, how not to do it, doesn't help. And if you're the 45-year-old child of a 68-year-old parent, you find yourself interacting with your parent only on a "duty and obligation" basis (and sometimes end up avoiding the parent entirely) so you won't get "parented" to death.

This is a sad state of affairs, for there is often a great depth of love and caring between parents and children that gets lost when parents don't move from parenting their grown children into treating them like adults; in a word, when parents fail to grow beyond the parent role.

As your parent's child, however, you have great power. Yes, there are some parents who truly don't care about their kids, but that's not the majority. Most of us have great power when it comes to our parents, because they don't want to lose us. Use that power to your advantage. Help your parent grow up.

How to do this? Well, all of us have within us a child, adolescent, parent, and adult portion—you as well as your parent. Usually when your parent "parents" you, you find yourself dumping into child mode, either submissively and passively agreeing to whatever, or stubbornly digging in your heels in good two-year-old fashion, saying "no" to anything and everything, regardless of its validity. Instead, kick into adult mode, which will encourage your parent into responding from his "adult" mode.

Adult mode relies basically on five key words/phrases: what, how, how much, where, when. For example, your parent says: "You shouldn't eat ice cream, it'll ruin your figure." You reply in adult mode: "What is it about ice cream that will ruin my figure?" Parent: "It'll make you fat." You, remaining in adult mode: "How much ice cream do you think I'd need to eat to make me fat?" Parent (by now getting annoyed or bored, this isn't going the way she's used to): "I don't know, just don't eat it." You, still maintaining an adult mode: "I enjoy being trim and fit. I've figured I can have X grams of fat per week and maintain my health and figure. Thank you for your concern, but I'm still well within my ice-cream quota for the week." Big silence.

This is not putting down your parent. This is training your parent that if she would like to have a conversation with you regarding ice cream, that's fine, you have thoughts to share with her and are happy to have her input. However, if your parent just wants to tell you how to live your life, sorry, you're doing that just fine on your own.

Notice in all this, you're really growing up yourself, too. You can't have adult conversations with your parent until you've formulated your own opinions and values. So it's really a win-win. By encouraging your parent to adopt an adult mode, you get yourself there too.

> We've had bad luck with our kids—they've all grown up.
>
> CHRISTOPHER MORELY

4

Quit Rescuing, Start Empowering

You're trying to get your work done, you've got this particularly problematic situation you need to deal with, you're under a deadline, and every two minutes, your coworker is bugging you, saying "I'm having so much trouble with this, this is the most miserable project, and you always seem to do this stuff so easily . . ." as he trails off, hoping you will, as you so often do, say, "OK, all right, just leave it here and I'll handle it," meanwhile knowing you really shouldn't do his work for him, you have piles of your own to do, but it just seems easier and faster to get rid of him by (once again) doing it yourself.

Or . . . your sibling/mate/parent is having a dickens of a time sorting out which HMO provides the best benefits, or which career path is the most suited to her, or which plumber to use, and you really have better things to do than sit there while she moans and groans, and, besides, she argues with you as you try to give her ideas that really makes you nuts, and you give up and just say "I'll do it for you," and there you are saddled with yet another responsibility in an overly responsibility-filled life.

So now what? You can't very well dump all your friends and family with a "Well it's your problem, tough luck, I'm outta here" attitude, but you can't keep doing it all for them either. You can, however, empower them to do it for themselves, to give them support and ideas about how to get to where they want to go rather than doing it for them.

5

1. Acknowledge the situation and empathize with their feelings about the situation: "Gosh, that sounds like a really challenging project," "That's a tough decision to make," "You're having a hard time with this."

2. Put the problem squarely back in their laps: Your coworker says "You always seem to do this stuff so easily," hoping to guilt you into doing it for him. Don't take the bait, respond with (for example) "Yes, I do. I really worked at it/read up on it/practiced it to get good at it. You can do that too."

Or, for example, your sibling/mate/parent is bemoaning his lack of ability to make the HMO/career/plumber decision. Resist doing it for him, and empower them with: "You made a great decision with X. You can figure this out just as you did with X."

3. Become a resource person rather than a "do-it" person. Empower people by suggesting the resources they can use themselves; show them the way rather than doing it for them: to your coworker, "There's a great manual on X in the storeroom/the company will pay for training in Y," etc. To your sibling/mate/spouse: "The HMOs often have a help hotline available/there are a number of career counselors in the phone book, you can interview them to see which ones you like," etc.

Strangely, in the end, people will resent you for doing it for them when they are basically capable of learning how to do it for themselves. Serve those you care about and yourself better by showing them the way rather than carrying them down it.

> We don't know who we are until we see what we can do.
>
> MARTHA GRIMES

A Magical Question

You wake up, you drag yourself out of bed, stumble over to the sink, take one look at yourself in the mirror, and groan: "Oh, this is gonna be a bad hair day, I can tell, my cowlick is standing straight up and it'll never stay put like I want, I'll bet I forgot to buy some coffee, and even if I still have some, it probably won't be any good anyway, been in the freezer too long." You then flip on the radio, and here you go again: "Listen to that, the freeway traffic is miserable and I'll bet it's gonna drizzle today, just my luck, the car will probably fail to start and I'll have to wake up the neighbors to jump start me and they'll hate doing it and then I'll be late to work," and at about this point it's all you can do not to crawl back into bed, pull the covers up over your head, and stay there until some time next year.

Anything you focus on grows. This simple statement contains a great truth. Numerous experiments have been conducted in which identical plants placed in identical conditions of soil, water, and sunlight were simply talked to differently. ("Talked to?!" Yes, talked to.) Plant #1 was told what a miserable failure it was and how it would never make it as any kind of decent plant. Plant #2 was talked to very neutrally, and plant #3 was told what a glorious and beautiful plant it was and how splendidly it would grow. Guess what? Plant #1 hardly grew at all, plant #2 did OK, and plant #3 THRIVED!

You can't go through your day focusing on everything that could possibly go wrong and expect to have a happy, fruitful day. It just won't happen. Anything you focus on grows. Guaranteed. So here's a question to focus on that will bring magic into your life:

What could go right today?

Think about it. What would your day be like if you woke up, dragged yourself out of bed, stumbled over to the bathroom sink, took one look at yourself in the mirror, and said: "Hey, my cowlick's up! Maybe today, it'll stay in place, maybe that new mousse I bought will work, gee, I may have remembered to buy coffee, and if I didn't, maybe a cup of tea would do the trick." You flip on the radio and continue: "Listen to that, the freeway traffic is miserable, I might be able to use surface streets to get around it, and I'll bet it's gonna drizzle today, good, I can try out my new raincoat, the car might start 'cause it's not really that cold out, and boy am I lucky to have neighbors willing to help me out if I need a jump start, I'll bet I'll even make it to work on time."

Now, at about this point life doesn't look so bad and instead of crawling back in bed, you make the bed and are ready to face the day.

So much of your happiness is dependent on your point of view. If you persist on looking for everything that can go wrong, it will. And if you persist on looking for everything that can go right, it will too. Believing that the negative is more likely to happen than the positive is foolish: Focus is focus; it's not whether it's negative or positive that matters, it's how much of it you do. Hone your positive focus in with laser-like intensity and watch the magic in your life grow!

Experience is not what happens to a man; it is what a man does with what happens to him.

ALDOUS HUXLEY

Stop, Look, and Listen

You're positively annoyed. You've asked the secretary three times to please get a certain piece of work done, and nothing's happening. You have 22 other things on your mind, and the last thing you need is incompetent help. You tell the secretary, "Look, I need this work done, and I need it done now," and she bursts into tears. You now feel guilty in addition to feeling annoyed.

You get home, your kid hasn't done any of his chores and is moping around whining "I'm starving, when's dinner?" Remembering the secretary bursting into tears, you don't yell, you clamp down hard on your emotions, and say with a false sweetness, "As soon as you've done your chores," and he wails, "That's not fair!" and runs into his bedroom, slamming the door on the way. You give up. "It doesn't matter if I yell, or if I'm nice, I can't win," whereupon you plunge into a full quart of Häagen-Dazs and don't stop 'til you're eating cardboard.

Well, actually, you can win; you just have to know what the game is. The game you're playing at the moment could be called "Me, me, me," whereas a more effective game would be "Me, them, me." Notice you still get top billing.

In other words, take into account where the other person is coming from. Whenever things aren't going your way, when people seem to refuse to do what you need them to do—stop, look, and listen.

1. *Stop.* Stop what you're doing or asking for as soon as you realize things aren't happening the way you want them to.

2. *Look.* Look around you. Literally and figuratively. Look at what seems to be going on with the person, what you may be contributing to the situation, what else is going on in the environment.

3. *Listen.* Ask the person what is going on, and LISTEN to what he says. Take it into account, work with it.

For example, after the second time the secretary didn't do your task, STOP; figure something is wrong here. LOOK (as in observe): Is your secretary ill, preoccupied, deluged with work? Have you asked her to do work beyond her skill level, too much, below her status, not in her work description, unfamiliar? Then, LISTEN: Ask her if there's something about the task that doesn't work for her, or if she has a concern she needs to let you know about, and then listen attentively to what she has to say.

With your child, similarly, STOP: Remind yourself it's unusual for him not to have done any of his chores. LOOK: Does he look feverish, tired, out of sorts, is there something you've asked of him that's out of the ordinary, did you have words before separating for the day? Then LISTEN: Ask how your kid is, what's going on, what happened in his day, and (pointing out that it's unusual for him not to do any chores) ask gently why he didn't do them, and then listen as openheartedly as possible to what he tells you.

Stop, look, and listen. An amazingly simple yet amazingly effective technique. Use it and be surprised at how much more easily and thoroughly things get done!

> *T*he great aim of education is not knowledge but action.
>
> HERBERT SPENCER

How to Change—For Real

Did you ever wonder why it's so hard to change sometimes? Why, for example, once you've gotten yourself on a great new diet-and-exercise program, you find yourself "slipping" and having things go back to the way they were? Why, when you've managed to keep your office/home functioning smoothly for a month, that things start unraveling and you find yourself back in a constant state of emergency and damage control? And you find yourself saying things to yourself like: "Well, it's because I'm lazy," or "I just don't have any will power," or "I'll never amount to anything, I can't even keep my desk neat"?

Unfortunately, blaming and putting yourself down isn't helpful. All it does is hurt you, and you're still left with your original problem. After all, you really do want to be healthier and more fit/keep your home/office running smoothly. So consider this: Maybe what's going on isn't about what a terrible bad person you are, but about the terrible bad *image* you have of yourself.

Image precedes reality. In other words, you can't have that fit body, organized desk, etc., unless you can first imagine it. Oh, you might be able to have it for a while, but you won't be able to sustain it, to have it "for keeps." Before you try to create the change you want in your life, create the image.

1. Acknowledge your current image of whatever it is you wish to change. You can't create a new image if you don't know what the existing image is. For example "I see myself as a flabby and out-of-shape person" or "I see myself as this perpetual whirlwind, always in motion, papers flying, too much to do, no time to clean things up or make things neat."

2. Acknowledge your image of the idea of change. This is very important! If your image of "change" is of something nigh onto impossible, taking incredible will power, always involving struggle and hardship, why in the world would you want to do it?

3. Acknowledge your image of yourself relative to change. Do you welcome change? Do you see yourself as someone who drops outdated habits and creates new ones easily? Or do you see yourself as someone for whom change is difficult, painful, and largely unsuccessful?

4. Here comes the good part: Change your image of yourself relative to change. If you don't like who you are relative to change, start seeing yourself differently. You may wish to start slowly with this, for example, "I am willing to be good at changing things" before you move onto "I find change easy and comfortable" to "I enjoy change."

Use these statements as affirmations you repeat many times daily to help you change your image. Use the same process to then change your image of the idea of change ("Change is great, change is easy!"), and finally, create the new image you wish to bring into your life: Really see yourself as the person you wish to be, experience living life that way in daydreams and meditations, start to think and feel and respond as a person having/being those things you want to think and feel.

NOW you have excellent chances of creating whatever it is you want—for real! Enjoy!

> *T*he unfortunate thing . . . is that good habits are much easier to give up than the bad ones.
>
> W. SOMERSET MAUGHAM

Surviving Stress

Stress is a big part of our lives, and if we don't know how to deal with it in appropriate and healthy ways, it can kill us—physically as well as emotionally and spiritually. When you find yourself in a stressful situation, ask yourself the following questions, and use the suggested techniques to help you survive stress successfully.

1. Where's my attention? What are you paying attention to? You have to recognize what's going on before you can change it. Ask yourself: "Am I focusing on how anxious/depressed/upset/angry I am about the situation or am I focusing on dealing with it?"

2. If you're focusing on how you're feeling (how anxious/depressed/upset/angry you are), own what you're feeling and then release it.

Give your feeling a name: it's not just "stress," it's "fear that I'll lose my job," or "anger at my spouse." Be willing to release that emotion. This can be difficult. It's often comforting to cling to hurt or upset feelings, as in: "I'll sit here in my cave for a day/a week/a month or two, and lick my wounds." Short-term (an hour or so), that's fine, but beyond the very short-term, clinging to a feeling is problematic. It doesn't solve anything, and it doesn't in the long run make you feel any better.

Use the 20-minute release technique to fully let go of your uncomfortable feelings: Take 20 minutes and either talk your unhappy feeling out loud into a mirror until you're totally and utterly done, or write it out until you've literally written every bit of it out, or beat it out of a pillow (safely, please!) until you're spent, or cry it out until there are no tears left. If you're really committed and intense about releasing, you'll find 20 minutes are plenty. Once you've released the feelings, you're ready to handle the problem.

3. Ask yourself: "Is this something I can problem solve?" If yes, figure out what you need to do and do it. For example, if your stress comes from having too much work to do, learn how to delegate work, create more efficient work habits, learn to set limits on what you'll accept to do, etc.

If no, change your perceptions. Baring catastrophic situations, which isn't what we're talking about here, a situation isn't stressful until it's perceived as such. For example, for some people flying in an airplane is a joy, for others it's a fearful, stressful experience. Stress can be thought of as stimulation perceived as painful. Change your perception of what is and isn't painful. Is this just mind games? No, it's altering your point of view to enable you to get to a place where you can either problem solve or no longer experience the situation as stressful: "There's too much to do" becomes "Thank God I have a job to do/home to run!" Once you've changed your perception, you can get into problem solving (delegate/hire more help/become more efficient, etc).

4. Be proactive: Know what causes stress for you and deal with it *before* it becomes a problem. That way you will greatly decrease the amount of stress with which you'll ever have to deal.

The less you allow stress to run your life, the freer you are to enjoy your life—and that's the whole idea, isn't it!

Happiness is not a reward, it is a consequence. Suffering is not a punishment, it is a result.

ROBERT G. INGERSOLL

When Silence Isn't Golden

You're in the heat of a terrible argument with your sibling/friend/ spouse. You burst into tears and confess your most vulnerable feelings, literally pouring your heart out, and when you're done, in the silence that follows, through your sobs, you ask him, "Please say something, anything"—and he just stands there mute. "Oh, I can't believe you won't say anything, after all I've just told you, you're horrible!" you cry out, running from the room to throw yourself across the bed, thinking how could anyone be so heartless.

Well, maybe he's heartless, but chances are, he just didn't hear you. "Didn't hear me," you wail, "but I was talking perfectly clear and loud and there's no way he didn't hear me." And yet in all likelihood, I assure you, he didn't hear you.

You see, hearing is done not just with the ears. Hearing is done with the mind. And many people, when in the presence of someone fraught with emotion, cease to hear the other. It's as if when your emotion is so powerful, it takes up all the other person's attention and energy at the time, and he has none left over for the words. He even has none left over to tell you, "Hey, I can't hear your words past your emotion"—if he is aware of what's going on at the time, which is unlikely.

This is equally true of anger. In broad terms, anger and tears are the two emotions that seem to take up the most attention/energy from the listener. The more agitated or stormy the anger/tears, the more difficult for people to listen to the words.

"So what are you telling me, that I can't get angry or cry when I have something important to say?" In a word, yes. Certainly get angry, cry, express yourself emotionally as feels necessary and right for you— just don't try to talk at the same time! So many women, in particular, think their husbands are emotionless blobs, when what's really going on is that, generally speaking, men are incapacitated by tears. Their minds turn off hearing anything, and they will either say things they don't really mean or say nothing at all, in order to cope. So, using tears as a ploy is ineffective. In the short run, he may give you anything you want, but in the long run, he didn't really hear a word you said and won't be able to genuinely respond to what was going on for you.

Women, in general, are incapacitated by anger. When a man comes at us with violence or threat of violence, our brains go on hold. It's all we can do to grab on to, "How do I defend/protect myself here?" The thought of actually listening at that point in time is impossible.

Certainly these are generalizations. Many women don't cope well with tears, and many men can't listen past anger. But it might help you better understand your significant other if you take this generalization into account.

Respect your emotions. Express them in appropriate ways, absolutely. Then, when you are calm and able to do so with minimum emotion, talk. And talk and talk. Say it all; for now, you will be heard.

The most incomprehensible thing about the world is that it is comprehensible.

ALBERT EINSTEIN

Handling Fear

How many times have you wanted to make a change in your life, only to say to yourself, "But what if?" And out comes a litany of your fears: "What if I leave my job and can't find another one—oh, my gosh, I'll starve to death, I'll be a homeless person, I'll die," or "I can't leave my spouse, what if nobody else ever loves me? I mean rotten love is better than no love, at least I know what I'm dealing with," or "I can't go for an AIDS test! What if I find out I'm HIV positive, that's it, my life would be over, I'm too scared!"

Caught in the maelstrom of your fears, you don't do anything. You stay with the job you hate that neither challenges your creativity nor rewards your talents; you stay with the spouse who has little if any respect for you and regards you as a possession to be whopped around or an object to manipulate at will; you won't take an AIDS test, but you look at every physical symptom you have as possible evidence of AIDS and are riddled with anxiety.

Not a pretty picture, and yet so many of us, so much of the time, allow our lives to be run by FEAR rather than *handling the fear* and allowing our lives to be run by *choice, self-respect, and self-love.* Instead of getting paralyzed in that place of fear whenever you want to make a change in your life, recognize that you are scared, forgive yourself for being scared (it's one of the instinctual emotions that serves us well in certain life-threatening conditions), and be willing to handle your fear.

How do you do that? By weeding out those fears that are absurd and dismantling those that are real.

1. *Weeding out the absurd fears.* Do you really believe in your heart that if you leave this job you will never ever find another one and will starve to death? Probably not. Are you 100 percent convinced that you are so unlovable that you will never ever find another person to love you should you leave this miserable relationship? Well, maybe not 100 percent, may be 95 percent convinced. Are you positive that you not only have AIDS but that there is literally no hope whatsoever should you be so diagnosed? Well, maybe you're not really fearful you have it, you just don't want to find out if you do. Be truthful with yourself. Sort out what are the absurd fears, meaning those with little genuine foundation, and which are the real fears, or the portion of your fears that feel real to you.

2. *Dismantle those fears that remain.* Ask yourself: "Which part of me is scared? The inner child who feels powerless? The parent part of me that wants me to do things the way I 'should,' or would rather sit here blaming and judging me for 'failing' at my relationship rather than letting me move on? What are my belief systems here? Do I believe in a nasty, hostile world where there is so little love and joy I'll never get any? Why do I believe I'll never get any?" Work with the parts of you that stop you from growth, work with the beliefs you hold that get in your way. Dismantle your real fears by removing the beliefs and attitudes that hold them in place.

For example, it may seem difficult to find a new job, but if you focus on those qualities and talents you have that could serve others, you will indeed find that you do have what it takes to do work you love. If the real fear that remains in leaving your relationship to find a more positive one is that you may have to face loneliness for a while, then look to ways to secure support systems for yourself while you're creating that new loving relationship. Certainly if you are HIV positive, you

20

have NO chance of healing or living with as much dignity and quality as possible if you don't find out your status rapidly.

In other words, don't let fear stop you. It isn't fear that stands between you and your joy, it's your willingness to *let that fear stand unchallenged* that gets in the way. Everyone gets scared. The only difference between successful people and others is that successful people don't let the fear stop them. Value yourself: Love yourself enough to free yourself from your fears and make more positive choices for yourself.

> *Failure is the opportunity to begin again more intelligently.*
>
> HENRY FORD

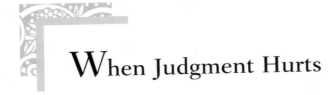

When Judgment Hurts

It's so tempting, when things go wrong, to panic and assume that things are going to go only from bad to worse: "Oh, no, I just lost my job, how awful, I'm gonna be a homeless person, it's a terrible economy, how am I ever going to find another job?" or "She left me, how horrible, I'm going to be all alone and no one will ever love me again, I'm terrible at relationships, I drove her off, I know it," or "That's it! I've no choice, I'm gonna have to declare bankruptcy, I'm going to lose my house, my car, how am I ever going to hold my head high again? How will I ever get credit? This is the worst thing that ever happened to me," and, indeed, these situations are all painful. But where you get in trouble isn't with the pain of the original situation, it's with how you get stuck on that pain.

The problem isn't that you lost your job or your significant other or your assets, the problem is that you define that loss as bad and then hammer yourself with that judgment. Seeing the event as bad, you now proceed to see all future events as bad and yourself (usually) as bad, too, for letting the whole thing happen.

Now you're in a bind. You can't move backward (what's done is done), but you can't get yourself motivated to move forward because you've immobilized yourself by judging the event and its consequences as bad and all future outcomes as bad. So you get depressed or angry and live in a blue funk until somehow the whole thing passes (you hope).

There is a more elegant way. Take the judgment off. Acknowledge the painfulness of the situation without judging it as "bad." "Bad" only stops all movement, all flow. It serves no other useful purpose. Do you then judge the situation as "good"? No, that would be ludicrous! In the preceding examples, you're in pain over these losses; how could you then describe them with any honesty as "good"? Just take the judgment off—all judgment. See the event for what it was—painful; acknowledge and mourn your loss, then DECIDE CONSCIOUSLY how you'd like to weave that event into the fabric of your life.

For example: "OK, I lost my job. Well, since I'm starting fresh, let me look around and see what I'd really like to do. What talents do I have that would be valued in the present economy, what environment would I thrive in, what education/training would be helpful now?" or "Although I lost my significant other, and I'm sad over that, I didn't lose 'love' in the larger sense. I can still give and receive love with my friends, family, pets, etc. This might be an opportunity to look at the place of 'love' in my life overall, how I define 'love,' and whether I do want a relationship at this time and what kind? And look at how I can be more loving toward myself and therefore toward others. . . ." And similarly with the bankruptcy example: "No, I'm not happy I'm bankrupt, but how can I make this event work for me, create more happiness in my life from right here right now?"

Life is an experience, not a contest. Take whatever events come along and work with them to keep growing in love, joy, and success. Judgment stops that growth, so don't give up the growth, give up your judgments!

---

*S*ometimes the best gain is to lose.

GEORGE HERBERT

Anger: Dumping vs. Dealing

You're having an absolutely lousy day at work. Your boss is being entirely unreasonable, expecting you to be in three places at once, and when you do exactly what she asked you to do, she bawls you out. When you try (biting your tongue very hard so as not to scream) to gently(!) point out that you were only following her directives, you get yelled at even louder! At this point there is nothing you would like better than to scream bloody murder, grab your boss by the throat, and throw her bodily out the window. As a matter of fact, you'd even settle for just telling her off, as long as you could do it at top volume. But, no, that little voice within you kicks in: "Now, this is your boss, she could fire you, and then where would you be?" and so you just sigh, squashing all those feelings . . .

Then when you get home and your spouse/child forgets to get dinner, set the table, or whatever other responsibility was his that day, again all you want to do is slaughter him, but again that little voice says: "You can't do that—you're a good person, good people don't slaughter others, so he forgot, what's the big deal? Besides, if you yell at him, maybe he won't love you anymore, and maybe you aren't that good person you think you are, maybe you're really just a horrible, angry, abusive person," and so you sigh, squashing all those feelings.

As saintly as it might seem, squashing angry feelings may end up killing you. There is a high correspondence between stuffed angry feelings and resentment—and cancer. Stuffing feelings leads to heart attacks, ulcers, and various other highly unpleasant conditions.

"But, Dr. Noelle, I don't want to go around dumping my anger all over people!" Of course you don't, that would be highly inappropriate. Huh? *Dumping* would be inappropriate; *dealing* with your anger is appropriate. Dumping would consist of yelling at your boss/spouse. Dealing with your anger consists of expressing that same anger in a safe, appropriate manner and then communicating it safely and appropriately.

1. *Express your anger.* Expressing your anger safely is most easily and effectively done either through writing your feelings in the form of a letter *you never send,* writing your feelings in your private journal, beating the sh.. out of a pillow safely placed in the middle of your bed (pillow named boss/spouse/whatever), or in meditation. The first three methods are fairly self-explanatory. Expressing your anger in meditation (my personal favorite) is done as follows: Sit in a quiet, comfortable room where you won't be disturbed for about 20 minutes (no phones, etc.). Close your eyes, relax your body, take three deep calming breaths. Then picture in your mind's eye your boss/spouse/whoever and yell at him/her. Say whatever it is you have to say, get physical with him/her if that feels right, beat him/her up, tear his/her arms and legs off, roll him/her in the mud. *You cannot harm another being in meditation IF your intent is to release anger.* If your intent is that when you are done with the meditation, that person will be crippled for life, STOP! Wrong intent. As long as you are clear that your intent is release of anger, all is well. Keep releasing until you feel "spent," then take a nice deep breath, open your eyes—and there, you're done! No repressed stuffed anger to hurt you, and no yelling all over your boss at your workplace or spouse at home where it could hurt both of you.

2. *Communicate.* Now that you've released the anger, figure out what you need to *say* to your boss/spouse/child. Make it specific, direct, and goal oriented. By that I mean, don't be out for revenge or to make yourself "right." That won't work. Figure out what you want and

25

go for that: "Boss, I'm confused. I want to do a good job for you, but I'm unclear as to what you want done first. Please tell me." "Boss, I want to do a good job for you, but I can't hear you when you raise your voice." Be willing to negotiate to get what you need. (Negotiate means get creative so that all parties get what they need, not give up what you/they want.)

> *It's not true that nice guys finish last. Nice guys are winners before the game ever starts.*
>
> ADDISON WALKER

What Now? Why Me?

You're driving down the freeway—it's a nice bright sunny day—totally minding your own business, when, POW! your engine blows up, and OK, you got out of the car in time, but now you're standing at the side of the road, looking at your rapidly dying vehicle, thinking, "Now what? This is terrible, how am I going to get a new car? Why now? Why me?" You're perfectly happy in your job, doing something you enjoy with congenial coworkers and a decent environment, and WHAM! the economy forces the company out of business, and you're "downsized" out of a job: "Now what? How am I going to get work? In this economy?" The relationship you thought was going so well, you suddenly find out he's had a change of heart, he needs to go off and "find himself," only that "finding" somehow doesn't include you. Again, the same questions: "Why now? Why me?" and "Now what?"

Anytime something leaves your life, it's an opportunity for something new and potentially much better to enter your life. As difficult as it may be to see and appreciate the potential for something better to come into your life when you are in the throes of your car/job/relationship falling apart, that something better is there, waiting for you to reach out to it, when you are ready. And the way to reach out to the wonderful new is not by denying the hurtful reality of your loss, but rather by *fully allowing your loss,* so you can genuinely and successfully move on.

You see, the long-term damage to one's life isn't caused so much by the loss itself, as it is by our *hanging on to the feeling of loss*. People hang on to the feeling of loss because they never allow themselves to really get in touch with their feelings about that loss. Instead they allow themselves to feel a little bit all the time, which means they drag the loss around forever, never leaving room for the new to come in. If you are willing to deeply feel, mourn, and grieve your loss, then you will be in a position to fully *release* the loss and look for the wonderful new.

1. *Feel, mourn, and grieve.* Feel and express your feelings safely and appropriately. Having your world blow up in your face like that, especially when you thought all was going well, *does* feel awful. You don't need to get into the feelings of self-pity, the "oh, poor me, ain't it awful" so much, as the *real* feelings that lie underneath: the ANGER at your world blowing up, at the person(s) you hold responsible, at the universe, at the guardian angel that failed to guard you (don't worry, she knows you're mad anyway), at the world, at whatever it is you need to rail. Allow yourself to feel the DISAPPOINTMENT, the HURT, the SADNESS that lies underneath. Give yourself permission to mourn and grieve the passing of something important in your world. Once you feel you have expressed all the feelings you had about the loss, move on to step 2.

2. *Open to the possibility of something new.* You can't bring something into your life unless you first acknowledge the *possibility* of that something happening. This may take some work! Sit quietly with yourself and look at what your beliefs are in this area. Do you think the current state of the economy jeopardizes your chances of a good job? What about the fact that some people are making more money every year? Do you believe that you will never find such a good relationship again? You didn't know *this* relationship existed until it happened! Do you believe you'll have all sorts of difficulty finding the money for a new car? What does this say about your beliefs in your creativity and

resourcefulness? Be willing to examine your beliefs in the area of your loss sincerely and change whatever limiting beliefs you find into beliefs that do not limit you, but rather open you to the possibility of something new—and better—coming into your life.

Now you're ready to move on to *creating* that something new, free of the encumbrance of old resentments and hurts. Dream, vision, see what you want as vividly as you can, and take the steps to getting it. Go for it! *Now* you can get it!

> *If* you can imagine it, you can achieve it; if you can dream it, you can become it.
>
> WILLIAM ARTHUR WARD

I'm Bored!

You're at your job, doing whatever it is that you do at your job, be that in an office, at a construction site, or in a home, and you're bored. I mean, here you are, doing the same things day in and day out, and a great cry wells up in you, "I'M BORED!" You go home, feed the cat/dog/child, get dinner, turn on the tube—and it's the same old programs done in the same old way and again, you feel that restless gunky feeling—BORED! There's nothing in the mail but junk, your mate/date is their same-o same-o self, and you go to bed depressed, thinking: "Is this all there is?" You don't particularly want to say anything to anyone because the last time you made that mistake, all you got was: "What are you complaining about, geez, you should have *my* job—crisis city! I'd love to be bored," and "You're bored? Great—I've got some stuff needs doing, you can do it. Believe me, you get enough going, you won't be bored," missing the point entirely. It's not that you're not busy, you're plenty busy, there's always more to do, it's that—you're bored.

Boredom is clearly different from hanging out, being relaxed, just enjoying whatever is around you. Boredom is draining, it is life depleting. Behind boredom there is an anxiety, a strange restlessness that gnaws at you.

Yet boredom sounds so innocuous, those who aren't don't give it any credence at all. After all, people don't kill out of boredom, they don't beat their children out of boredom, they don't do drugs or other addictions out of boredom—or do they? . . . They do. We all do. It's when you're bored that you open the freezer and take out the ice cream you really don't want to eat and eat the whole thing. It's when you're bored that you take that extra drink you really aren't that interested in. It's when you're bored that you find yourself playing silly mean games with your brother/the cat. Certainly, that's not the only reason you do these things; at other times you might do such things out of other motives, but boredom is unfortunately a primary and often overlooked source of self (and other) destructive behavior.

"OK, fine," you say, "I understand that boredom can lead to such awful things, but what can I do about it? I've tried keeping busy, but that doesn't work."

You're right, it doesn't. Oh, it works up to a point, certainly sitting on your behind all day is going to be boring, and getting up and getting busy helps, but the bottom line is, boredom isn't about getting busy. There are some very not-busy people who aren't bored. Boredom is about—*not giving.* When you're not giving of yourself in whatever activity or moment you are living, you're susceptible to boredom. It doesn't matter what you do, doing it "by the numbers" is boring. For example, even if you do the same things in your job every day, you don't need to perceive them in the same way every day. You can choose to see them differently, giving to your job more of your talents, or different talents from what you usually do. Become more involved in how your job contributes to others, to the overall success of the company, to the bettering of your community. Seeing things differently allows you to experience them differently.

You're watching TV. You find yourself drifting into boredom no matter how many times you change the channels. Fine. So involve yourself, give of yourself to the program. Ask yourself, "Well, now, if I were that character in that situation, what would I do? If I were the writer, how would I have written that scene?" Compose a letter to the producers of the program telling them how their program fails to reflect life as it is, whatever, you get the idea, engage yourself in the process. I guarantee you won't be bored.

Boredom, left to grow and blossom, literally kills. But it doesn't have to. Use boredom for its most worthy purpose, as a warning sign that in some way you are not giving of yourself, not engaging, not involving your being in whatever you're living at the moment. Not only will you thrive, but you'll be delighted and surprised at how exciting and delightful life becomes.

> *There are no uninteresting things, there are only uninterested people.*
>
> GILBERT K. CHESTERTON

The Pull of the Familiar

You've been going along, things are just great with your mate/lover/friend, and you think, "Wow, this is really neat, this is terrific," and it is. But you start feeling antsy, a little anxious, although you can't see any reason for being anxious, so you just push it away. And then something happens—someone does some little thing—he forgets to take out the trash, she leaves her dishes in the sink—and WHAM! suddenly you're in the middle of World War III. And then things calm down, and although everything's shaky for a while, the relationship pulls together, things get really good again, and once again you think: "Hey, OK, how about that—maybe we're going to make it!" and as things stay great, oddly enough you start feeling a little anxious, and sure enough—WHAM! here comes something that in hindsight seems so idiotic, so small, but there you both are, back in the middle of World War III. Dismally, you conclude either that you are a failure, no way can you create a good relationship, or that the relationship is a failure, or that he/she is a failure. However you look at it, all you see is misery, and whether you stay in the relationship or get out of it, you're one unhappy camper.

What to do? Well, first notice that maybe you're wrong. Maybe there isn't failure here at all. Maybe the whole problem is, you're not used to success. You see, most of us are far more familiar with what to do in the event of a disaster than we are with what to do in the face of happiness. How much training did you get in school on "How to deal

33

with successful relationships and the maintenance of happiness"? How many articles in modern magazines are devoted to this idea? How often did your parents lecture you on the subject? How many seminars? Billboards? TV shows? etc. None. Oh, maybe an article here and a show there, but the vast preponderance of the emphasis in our culture is on problems—what to do when your relationship is on the rocks. And certainly that is extremely important. But you also need to know what to do with the success and happiness of your relationship, otherwise, as given in the preceding examples, when all is going wonderfully well you will get anxious and somehow reestablish the old status quo by making a mountain out of the next molehill that comes along.

That is because of the pull of the familiar. We are always more comfortable with what is familiar to us than with what is not. That is why, as is well-documented now, battered women too often stay in an abusive situation: The hurt you know is less frightening than the (potential) hurt you don't know. You know what to do when your relationship isn't going well: You try to communicate better, read self-help books, talk it over with friends, a therapist, you write in your journal, etc. What do you do when your relationship is going well? Good question. Certainly you enjoy it, but how do you grow it from there? How do you go from happiness to greater happiness?

In a word, carefully. With love and patience. First, value what you have. Then look for more and more to value and appreciate, both within the relationship and with your mate/friend. The quickest way to lose a relationship is to stop valuing it. The surest way to develop a successful relationship is to find more and more ways to value it and to do so with increasing depth. Deliberately create opportunities to explore the wonder of the relationship, to explore the fun of it. Set aside special time together, commit to it, make plans to do special things together, give the relationship importance. Treat your mate/friend as special all the time, express your appreciation of him/her openly, often; never take the happiness for granted.

Does this mean ignore whatever problems arise? No, of course not. But don't ignore the happiness either. When you feel that funny anxiety: "Things are going too well, when's the other shoe going to drop?" work with yourself, let yourself know your anxiety is simply coming out of the unfamiliarity of happiness, and that there doesn't have to be "another shoe."

> *Kind words can be short and easy to speak, but their echoes are truly endless.*
>
> MOTHER TERESA

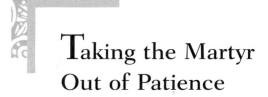

Taking the Martyr
Out of Patience

There's a definition of humility that I particularly like. It defines humility as the willingness to see everything new. Just because something was awful yesterday doesn't mean it has to be awful today. Just because something was wonderful yesterday doesn't mean it will be wonderful today. In both cases, it is up to us to create it the way we want it, to transform the awful into wonderful, the wonderful into even more wonderful.

"And what, Dr. Noelle, does this have to do with patience?" you ask. Good question. A lot, I'd say. You see, patience relies on trust. If you trust that the future of something will be good, then you have patience with it. For example, you're watching your rosebush grow. You trust that given the right nutrients, water, and care, it will grow beautiful roses. You are willing to be patient. Or, let's say you've been having problems with your kid. He's talking back and being snotty and in general being a pain. But you know that your kid's a good kid, and you trust that he is going to turn out all right. So you're patient. You're willing to take the time and do what it takes to help your child get on a happier track. Take the reverse situation. The clerk at the dry cleaner's is always losing stuff. She can never find your clothes using your dry cleaning slip, she has to root through racks and racks of cleaning, she drives you nuts. Your trust in the future of a satisfying interaction with her is nil. You go in there ready for war. You have no patience whatsoever.

It takes patience to grow anything: a happy child, a beautiful rosebush, a successful relationship. Patience *not* as in "putting-up-with" things that are objectionable to you, but patience as "a willingness to see everything new"; in other words, patience as a direct function of trusting the future to be good. For example, your mother/mother-in-law was really nasty to you on her last visit. She criticized your cooking, commented on the dying hydrangea in the corner, and made pointed comments about how you discipline your child/pet. Ordinarily, you might come from a highly defensive place, having no trust that the next interaction with her is going to be good; you won't have the patience it would take to work things through. So you "make nice," put a lid on it, minimize the time spent with her, and in general just put up with her until she's (whew!) gone.

But if you are willing to be humble, to believe that just because yesterday's interaction with her was horrendous doesn't mean that the next one will be and you trust that regardless of present appearances the future can be good, you will be willing to be patient. You'll be willing to take her aside, for example, and say "Mom, we need to talk. I'm very uncomfortable with how you behaved toward me last time. I don't like being scrutinized and criticized. I want us to work out a way in which we can both express how we feel about the other and what the other is doing without either one of us feeling bad about it. Are you willing to work on this with me?" If she's willing, praise be, you have the possibility of a good relationship here. If she's not, then you can choose what you want to do with the relationship so that you do create a happy future for yourself. That may mean limiting the amount of time you spend with her. That may mean seeing her only in public places of her own choosing so she isn't given the raw material with which to criticize your way of life. That may mean any number of choices, the important thing being—*your future is your responsibility.*

Be humble. Be willing to let everything be new, every day, and use that willingness as the basis for your trust in a wonderful future.

From that foundation of trust, build a future for yourself that you enjoy, armed with the patience that trust engenders.

Patience is such a misunderstood virtue. All too often it is synonymous with martyrdom and sacrifice. Instead, make it synonymous with joy and happiness, use it as the wonderful tool it is—a loving eye on the future and a wonderful one at that.

> *He that can have patience can have what he will.*
>
> BENJAMIN FRANKLIN

Translate Your Negative Traits into Positive Qualities

You're waiting for your 20-year-old daughter (liberated at last from the family household and now living with a roommate in a tiny apartment) to finish getting ready so you can go to dinner together, and as you do, you absentmindedly straighten pictures on the wall, line up the magazines on the coffee table, and put the coasters back in a neat stack. Your daughter comes out, takes one look at what you've done, and groans, "Oh, Mom/Dad, you are such a perfectionist. Can't you just leave things alone?" You feel caught, embarrassed, laugh a little, but figure, "Well, heck, isn't that what parents do? Straighten things up?" And off you go to dinner.

As you wait for the cashier on the way out, you're straightening the cards on the cashier's desk, replacing a menu that's stuck out of order, and you don't even know you're doing it until your daughter says, "Mom/Dad! Will you cut it out! You're embarrassing me, just quit messing with everything." Your daughter thinking you are an embarrassment is nothing new, but nonetheless you feel bad about it and you stop, saying "So I like being neat, what's wrong with that?" "Neat? Right," says your daughter, "neat is one thing, Mom/Dad, obsessive is another." Great, another snide comment from the X generation.

But the next day, when you're at work, rearranging the piles on your boss's desk and he says "Boy, what a perfectionist you are—must be hard on your family," you remember how many similar comments you've heard throughout your life and you think, "Gosh, maybe I am a perfectionist, how awful, I must drive everybody nuts," and you proceed to berate yourself for being so nit-picky and vow to yourself "I will not be neat. I will not be a perfectionist, I'll just leave everything as it is." But of course you can't do that, it's part of who you are, which just makes you feel worse. Now you're depressed on top of feeling as if you're ruining things with friends and family, generally being a perfectionist downer.

The good news is—you *are* a perfectionist. It only sounds like bad news because up until now you haven't recognized it as such and therefore haven't been able to *channel* your perfectionism in positive and useful ways.

What, in fact, is perfectionism? It's attention to detail, a love of precision, a drive to have things in a certain order or arrangement. Now, inflicted on your friends and family, this could be torture, but channeled into a hobby, type of work, or area of personal interest, perfectionism is an absolutely wonderful asset! Think of just how valuable perfectionism is, for example, when making models of anything—from miniature aircraft to models used in movie making, how valuable perfectionism is in looking at microscopic slides of cancer cells, or airbrushing a photograph, in running a profitable cleaning service, or any number of other types of work or hobbies. So the challenge becomes not "How do I stop being perfectionistic/aggressive/longwinded/, etc.," but rather "How do I translate my seemingly 'negative' traits into positive qualities?"

When people repeatedly point out certain of your traits to you as being less than wonderful, or you become aware of them yourself, take a different point of view. Ask yourself, "How could this trait of mine be put to good use? Where can I channel this characteristic so that instead of being a source of aggravation to myself and others, it is instead a source of value and enhances who I am in the world?" If you can't figure it out, ask your friends and observe others who have similar traits but seem to be more productive or satisfied in their lives. How do they channel their potentially negative traits?

Do some research, assume you will find the positive worth to all your traits, and go for it. You may find life has a whole new zest to it when you find a genuinely good "home" for your up-until-now "negative" sides.

> $\mathcal{P}$*essimism never won any battle.*
>
> DWIGHT D. EISENHOWER

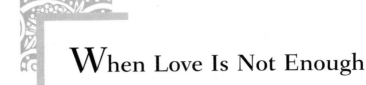

When Love Is Not Enough

You are "working" on your relationship. You have been working on this relationship as long as you can remember, as your friends are only too quick to remind you. In fact, it seems that every minute you are not actually at your job, you are in some way or other "working" on the relationship. Your relationship always seems somehow on the rocks; oh, there will be a good week or two, and then you're ecstatic. "He/she's really the one for me, everything's going great," and you bathe in a rosy glow, assuring everybody that, finally, you got it right, you know what to do, and ain't love grand. Until the next argument, cold shoulder, rejection, or other rupture in the fabric of your relationship, and there you are, dragging your boyfriend/girlfriend/mate back into therapy for the forty-seventh time that year (literally in the flesh, or figuratively in talking with your therapist), anxious and unhappy. "But, Dr. Noelle, I don't get it, I really really tried this time, I must just be relationship-impaired, there's no hope, I should just give it all up . . ." and so on, putting yourself down mercilessly.

Sometimes the problem isn't with what you do *in* a relationship. Many people are devoted, committed, and valiant in a relationship, genuinely putting their best foot forward, learning and growing, doing, as it were, "all the right things." Sometimes the problem is what you do *before* you get into the relationship. People tend to make two major errors in entering a relationship:

1. Failing to observe the person as he or she really is

2. Failing to be who they really are

Now, we all are "blind" to those we are attracted to—to a certain degree. And certainly everybody wants to put his or her best self forward at the beginning of meeting someone. So I'm not talking about 100 percent accurate observation, nor 100 percent being who you really are. However, there's a big difference between saying to yourself, "Oh, so he likes to hang with the guys and party all night, that's just because we're not together all the time yet; he won't need that kind of thing after we're really together," versus "Oh, so he likes to hang with the guys and party all night, maybe this person really needs that kind of down time with his friends." The latter is a realistic assessment of the situation, which may or may not be completely accurate, but at least takes into account what you are observing as really being that person's reality. When you say things like, "He won't need that kind of thing after we're really together," you're ignoring what that person's reality is and setting yourself up for a big surprise down the road.

1. *Observe, observe, observe.* Don't rush into a relationship. Take the time to observe the person and how he chooses to live his life rather than assuming somehow that will change or you can change him. Make an informed decision when you enter a relationship, "I know X, Y, and Z about the person, and I choose to accept these behaviors." This does not mean a partner does not change over time. He does, as you do! But don't count on such a change as you go into the relationship. Operate on the premise of "What you see is what you get," and be sure you've made lots of efforts to really "see" who the person is. You'll save yourself much "work" down the road.

2. *Be yourself.* As much as you can, be who you really are. If you like movies and hate water-skiing, don't suddenly decide, "Well, I could learn to love water-skiing, and I could go to movies with my friends instead." Perhaps you could, but in the interests of starting off a relationship with good chances of its being a happy and fulfilling one, better you should express who you are *at this point in time,* and let it be known that you are open to discovering other interests later on down the line. This is different from hiding who you are and hoping it will be OK to let your real self out once you're in the relationship. Do that and your companion is likely to feel betrayed, not overjoyed, and you are likely to feel frustrated and unhappy.

What you do in establishing a relationship is every bit as important as what you do during the relationship. Give equal attention to both and give yourself the joy of a truly fulfilling relationship.

> *W*ithout love, intelligence is dangerous. Without intelligence, love is not enough.
>
> ASHLEY MONTAGU

The Power of (All) Your Mind

When Freud figured out that there were layers to the mind and that often people behave not in function of what their conscious waking minds think, but rather in function of what their subconscious or unconscious minds think, he was on to an enormously powerful insight: There's a whole lot more going on than what sits in your everyday awake mind.

"So?" you ask. "That's nice, but what does that have to do with me?" *Everything.* You see, you may say to yourself, "I want a cushy job where I just rake it in. I want to be so rich, I could lose a million and I wouldn't feel a thing. I want to have the kind of job where I just sit back and collect the money. Matter of fact, clipping coupons and winning the lottery is my idea of the ideal job," but your subconscious or unconscious mind may hold beliefs such as: "Money is the root of all evil," "Rich people are cold and heartless," "I hate to dress up and you have to dress up, all the time when you're rich," "If you're rich, you never know if your friends like you for you or for your money." If that's the case, you will not get that job. Somehow or other, your subconscious or unconscious mind will see to it that you don't. After all, you don't want to be a cold, heartless person who has to dress up all the time and never knows who his true friends are! Or you may be wishing and hoping and longing for your true love to come along, but if your subconscious or unconscious mind holds the belief that "true love is a lie, it never happens," or "Kiss a frog, get a frog," what do you think the result is going to be?

There's nothing mysterious about this process, other than the fact that since most of us aren't in touch with those deeper layers of our mind, we don't realize they are there or how powerful they are. "Oh, great," you think, "so now I'm totally jinxed. Even if I want something and try really hard to get it, my subconscious or unconscious mind is going to somehow sabotage my efforts. Might as well give up right now!" No. Giving up is not the answer; your dreams and desires are what make you human. Instead, go about the necessary work of uncovering what those beliefs are that are keeping you from having those dreams come true, and changing them.

1. *Uncover your hidden beliefs.* Rather than jumping into the doing phase when you set your sights on a goal, start by taking some think-time. Sit with yourself, write the thing you desire at the top of a piece of paper, and then jot down any and all thoughts around that thing that comes to mind. It doesn't matter how silly or inconsequential or old-fashioned those thoughts and beliefs are: If you have them and they run counter to what you want, you need to uncover them! Don't try to argue yourself out of your thoughts, accept them for what they are—thoughts and beliefs coming out of your deeper levels of mind—and write them down.

Do this process over a period of a few days so that you don't miss any critical beliefs that may go unnoticed the first time you do it.

2. *Out with the old, in with the new.* The subconscious and unconscious mind respond best to symbols. To release your old unhelpful beliefs and create new ones, start by writing down all the beliefs you want to change and what the beliefs are you wish to put in place of the old ones. For example, "Money allows freedom and the opportunity to fulfill many desires" could replace "Money is the root of all evil." Then sit quietly by yourself and drift down into a meditative space, where you are in a room with a Book of Beliefs. Using your imagination as vividly as possible, engaging all your senses (sight, hear-

ing, touch, taste, smell, and your feelings), erase or otherwise destroy the old beliefs you find, all decaying and moldy, in your Book, and write in, with a beautiful flourish and great joy, your new beliefs. Once out of meditation, post those new beliefs where you can see them daily and repeat them to yourself as positive present-tense affirmations many times until they become as second nature to you as your old beliefs once were.

The power of mind is truly extraordinary—use it wisely for your greatest pleasure and happiness.

In the province of the mind, what one believes to be true either is true or becomes true.

JOHN LILLY

All You Have to Do Is Ask

It's late. You've had a long day. You get home, drop your things in a heap, and collapse on the couch. Your significant other, who got home way before you did, cries out "Hi, Hon!" in a pleasant voice from the other room. You would love nothing better right then than for your loved one to come in and ask "How are you doing? You look bushed. Can I do anything for you? Get you a cold drink?" But noooooo . . . At best, your significant other passes through the room on his way to the bathroom, asking "When's dinner?" or "Did you get the car fixed?" on his way.

You could kill. You do everything for this person, you're attuned to his slightest whim. If he complains of a headache, you fetch the aspirin; if he groans with fatigue, you say, "Poor baby," and rub his back; if he wants to spend the weekend away, you plan and strategize and scrimp and save and make it happen.

"When's it my turn?!" you yell (internally, of course), "He can see I'm lying here limp with stress, traffic, and overwork. Why doesn't he do something about it, like be nice to me, hold my hand, take care of me for a change?" And you hear Dr. Noelle's voice inside your head, "So, ask!" "I hate to ask," you reply, "I shouldn't have to ask! He should know what I want—it's not as if we just met. Besides I do for him all the time! All he has to do is the same things I do for him!"

"But," Dr. Noelle's voice presses on, "just for the sake of argument, what happens when you ask?" You hesitate, not wanting to give

48

in this easily, "Well, he generally does whatever it is I ask for." "Uh-huh," says Dr. Noelle, in that therapist tone you're all too familiar with, the one that says, "I thought so." "But I shouldn't have to ask!" you rail. "He should know what I want!"

Why? Why should your significant other know what you want? Or, more to the point, even if he does know in a general way what you like, why or how should he know what you want *when* you want it? Only you know that! And if, indeed, you seem to be more skilled at guessing what it is that he wants and are able to give it to him, why how nice for him! But, it still doesn't obligate your loved one to knowing what *you* want when you want it.

Wanting others to guess what's on your mind is crazy-making. If your significant other isn't good at it, he will end up feeling like a constant failure. If, indeed, your loved one does come through for you when you ask for whatever it is you need, then the phrase "I shouldn't have to ask" is magically and wondrously transformed to "All I have to do is ask!"

How delightful! How miraculous! All you have to do is *ask* for whatever it is you want and your loved one tries to get/do that for you. "But I've asked him for the same thing a hundred times!" you wail. So? Apparently whatever it is has a much lower priority for him than it does for you. So what? If he is willing to do that thing for you when you ask for it, stop resenting the asking! (If, indeed, he is unwilling to give you whatever it is you want, or does so grudgingly, then you need to sit down and talk about it; there may be other factors involved.)

Generally, when people resent having to ask for what they want, it's because they have difficulty expressing or owning their desires. If you feel guilty or undeserving about having something, then you'll want someone magically to just give it to you, which absolves you from having to face your feelings of guilt or undeservability. If you're unwilling to grow up and take responsibility for fulfilling your needs and desires, you'll want someone to behave like a parent and just give it to you.

Unfortunately, that puts you back in the position of a child, which although free of many responsibilities, is also minus a good many precious freedoms adults have.

Take responsibility! Be willing to ask for what you want and need. Hard as it is in the short run, it's much more fun in the long run. And start looking at your loved one with different eyes: How wonderful that all you have to do—is ask!

To love for the sake of being loved is human—to love for the sake of loving is angelic.

ALPHONSE DE LAMARTINE

Seven Ways Out of Depression

Your relationship is in the dumps, your job is about to be "downsized," the IRS has taken a sudden interest in you, and your best friend has just moved out of town . . . you're depressed.

You feel awful, you're tired all the time, yet you can't sleep at night; you either eat everything in sight, or throw up at the mention of food; nothing is fun anymore, everything hurts, you cry at the most unexpected times . . . you're depressed.

Depression may have any number of triggers that tip you into that horrid emotional pit where your world turns dark and bleak, but all of these have one underlying theme—loss.* Loss of health, loss of a child, loss of a job, potential loss of life (cancer, AIDS, accident)— yours or that of a loved one—loss of self-esteem, loss of success, loss of a cherished dream or hope, loss in all its different forms and to all its varying degrees. All these losses are familiar sources of depression. What is less obvious is the one loss common to all of these, loss of connection to your Soul, to the Life Force itself, to that which has been variously called God, Goddess, All That Is, Jehovah, the Light, the Christ, the Way.

---

*Some depressions are biochemically based and require medication. These suggestions are not meant to replace medication or any therapeutic or medical treatment.

51

That is why depression feels so awful, why the emptiness inside is so complete, so deadening. That's why admonitions to "Cheer up! Things could be worse!" or "What's wrong with you, just get positive!" don't work. Depression isn't just having a rough time. Depression is dis-connection from the very things that make life worth living: a sense of trust in a positive or benevolent future, a sense of power (your ability to manifest what you want in your reality), a sense of vision (being able to see a positive reality), and a sense of meaning (your purpose in life, the purpose of life itself). When you're depressed, none of that seems real: You don't trust the future to be good, you may not trust that there is a future! You don't have any confidence in your ability to make good things happen in your life, you see only sorrow and suffering all around you, and the "Meaning of Life" seems to be reduced to struggle and sweat; "Life's a bitch, and then you die."

But there is a way out. There is a way to reconnect to your Life Force, your Soul, to God, Goddess, All That Is, and through that reconnection, to lift yourself out of depression.

1. *Look to your beliefs.* You attract and allow experiences into your reality first and foremost according to what you believe. If you believe that "life is hard," then life will do its best to fulfill your belief. If you believe that one must struggle to prove one's worth, then struggle you will. If you believe that "love hurts," it will.

2. *Look to your feelings.* Be willing to feel. Depression is often a cover for anger, fear, even joy, you don't think you should have. Allow yourself, safely and appropriately (in meditation or in a journal are great places), to express ALL your feelings with gusto, no matter how ugly, no matter how beautiful. Then release those feelings. If you've truly felt and expressed them, you will be able to genuinely release them.

3. *Look to your secret fears.* The fears that wake you up in the middle of the night, those you hate to admit, even to yourself. What do

you really think is going to happen to you? "It will always be this way," "I'm going to die lonely, broke, and miserable," "I'll never find another love." Ask yourself: How are your fears trying to protect you? What are other ways you can protect yourself?

4. *Look to your dreams.* Do you have any? Or are you filled only with nightmares? And by "dreams," I don't mean night dreams, I mean "dreams" as in what you see for yourself, your loved ones, and our world. Dreams are what pull you forward. What's pulling you forward—anything? Dreams are what give you a sense of vision, of the possible. Whether you believe at this point in your depression that a Dream can come true is irrelevant—dream it anyway! The power of dream is phenomenal. It will pull you toward it as long as you see it, be that with your mental eyes in a visualization or with your heart.

5. *Look to your self-image.* How do you think of yourself? As victim, martyr, as always voted "least likely to succeed"? As winner, as "lucky," as average, as OK, as flawed? Your self-image colors how you view the world, and what you see is what you get—literally! If you see yourself as a victim, you will define what happens to you as proving your victim status. If you see yourself as a winner, you will define what happens to you as one step further on the winning path. (Does this mean people who are mugged or raped aren't victims? Of course not! But how they see themselves, as victims or as winners in life, determines how they deal with the situation and its impact.)

6. *Look for help.* "Ask and thou shalt receive" isn't just a pretty phrase. Ask! Ask for help from those who will respect your vulnerability. Look for support groups, community services, counselors, self-help books. Look for friends to give you ideas on how you can help yourself (not rescue you). And pray. However you conceive of prayer, be that talking to God, affirmations, chanting, meditation, walking in nature—pray. Ask for help from the All That Is. It is what gives us the breath of

life, what puts on this earth everything we need to be happy. It wants for us all good things.

7. *Look for the love.* You are loved. More than you will ever know, you are loved. Look for it in nature, feel the goodness of the sun on your face, of the earth beneath your feet, soak up the beauty of the ocean, of a sunset, feel the love all around you. Look for it on people's faces, in the cuddles of your pets, know it is there. Cultivate your love for yourself, find something you can love about yourself, no matter how small it may seem right now, and value that about you.

Depression may feel "forever," but it isn't. Look to the seven ways for guidance and let them lift you OUT of depression, into the light.

> *T*he last of the human freedoms—to choose one's attitude in any given set of circumstances, to choose one's own way.
>
> VICTOR FRANKL

Cinderella's Shoes

You've been looking for a good relationship for so long you'd just about given up, when this person comes along who's really nice, she treats you well and seems to care. "Gee," you think, this could be really great, and you conveniently ignore the fact that she likes hiking, bicycling, jogging, waking up with the birds, and thinking 10:00 P.M. is the middle of the night, when your preference is to read until 2:00 A.M., you've never heard a morning bird yet, and hiking is something you do to the refrigerator and back. You think, "Oh, heck, hiking is good for me, I don't mind," and cheerfully dump all the things you used to do that made you happy, in order to be with this person who you hope will make you happy. Six months down the road you wonder why you're so depressed. Your new girlfriend is as nice as ever, things are "fine"; you wonder, "What's wrong with me? Can't I ever be satisfied with anything? Why am I so depressed?"

Or, you've been let go from your job; the company's gone out of business. You never really did like your old job, so you're not too unhappy about it, but there you are, with a few months' worth of savings and a lot of worries about your future. You quickly grab the first job that comes along that offers decent pay, ignoring the fact that this new job is an awful lot like your old job, and once again wonder, some six or so months down the road, why you're so cranky and tired all the time, why you seem to be so—depressed.

You're suffering from a bad case of Cinderella's shoes. That's why. Do you remember in the fairy tale, before the Prince found Cinderella, how he asked all the women in the kingdom to try on the glass slipper? The two ugly stepsisters wanted to win the handsome Prince so much that they cut off pieces of their toes in order to fit into the glass slipper . . .

That's exactly what we do when we try to *make* ourselves fit into relationships or jobs or any other situations that aren't really for us, that force us to cut off pieces of our selves, our souls, in order to fit. Does this mean you can be in a relationship only with a clone of yourself or you can't take on a job that doesn't exactly meet your specific preferences? No, of course not. What it does mean is—be smart. Don't blind yourself to what the relationship or the job requires of you. Be conscious, be aware, and make informed decisions.

Say to the person you're attracted to, "I think you're great. I'd like for us to see more of each other, but I realize we have different needs and preferences, and I'd like us to talk about those." As scary as it may seem to openly discuss such differences, it is far less scary than the prospect of cutting off pieces of yourself for the sake of the relationship. After all, what kind of relationship is it if you allow only a portion of yourself to function in the relationship?

Before you take on a job or commit yourself to a situation (organization, hobby, etc.), ask yourself: "Does this situation fit with what I know about myself? Does this job, for example, satisfy *enough* of my work needs and preferences for me to be happy in it? Or, if it does not but I feel economically squeezed into accepting it, am I willing to look upon this job as temporary and take active steps to getting a job more suited to who I am?" Notice I did not phrase it as "getting a job for which I am more suited," which implies you have to fit yourself to the job, but rather the opposite: Focus on suiting the job to who *you* are.

Be willing to walk away. If, together, you and the person you are interested in cannot find ways for both of you to get *enough* of your

56

respective needs met, then be willing to let go of the relationship. If, after giving it plenty of thought and attention, you cannot see a way for you to exist as who you are in a job or other situation, don't commit to it. Walk away.

You cannot lead a satisfying and fulfilling life by filling your life with unsatisfying and unfulfilling experiences. Have the courage to stand up for what you want and need. Respect yourself. Trust that you will find a relationship or job that does fit you as you fit it—well enough for both to be satisfied. Don't sell yourself short. Cutting off toes never won the fair Prince!

> *You must first be who you really are, then do what you need to do, in order to have what you want.*
>
> MARGARET YOUNG

The Trap of Comparison

You're on yet another diet to try to lose those 15 pounds that seem determined to dog you until death do you-and-they part, and your trim and fit workmate bounds in after what appears to be an exhilarating jog, announcing a new record in low body fat . . . you hate him, but you hate yourself even more.

You've had to take a cut in salary (you feel lucky you still have a job), your benefits are being reduced monthly, and your next-door neighbor rushes over to tell you the oh-so-happy news: She has just landed a terrific, guaranteed, long-term contract with the hottest new industry in town, yes, and, oh, by the way, she is also getting married next week to a devoted and fabulously rich person. . . . Again, you feel the mixed emotions of "How nice for you, dear," "I hate your guts," and "WHY CAN'T IT HAPPEN TO ME?!" You then proceed to nurse your hostility into full-blown resentment.

Sound familiar? It's what happens to all of us whenever we fall into the trap of comparison. Comparing yourself with others will inevitably land you in one of two positions: better than ("Poor thing, I'm much better off/a better person than he is") or the more frequent position—victim ("Poor me, I'll never amount to anything/I can't do anything right"). Neither of these is a growth position. Both of them misuse the value that others' experience can have in our lives.

You see, everyone is on a different life track. Everyone has different hopes and dreams, even if superficially there may be resemblances. And each one of us is absolutely unique in terms of personality, background, and level of skill. When you think about it this way, comparing yourself with another is ridiculous—rather like comparing an orange to an apple and then being upset that oranges are juicy and apples crunch!

Comparing yourself with another is useful only if you use the comparison to help you stay and progress on your own life track. For example, your jogging friend is slim and trim: Although your definition of slim and trim is somewhat different from his, your life track includes slim and trim. Therefore, you use your evaluation of the jogger as an enviably slim person to ask him how he got to be slim and trim; in other words, you use this person as a RESOURCE to help you accomplish your goal. Now his "slim and trim" is useful to you: You are not using it to beat yourself up, you are using that evaluation to further your goals. Your neighbor is doing great in the work and romance worlds: terrific! Use her as a resource person, find out how she did it, and see if her way or any portion of it fits for you in your unique life track.

You have only so much energy to accomplish your dreams and desires in this lifetime. How much more valuable to use it furthering the success of your own life track rather than wasting it in "poor them" or "poor me"!

> *While one person hesitates because he feels inferior, the other is busy making mistakes and becoming superior.*
>
> HENRY C. LINK

The Fallacy of Control

The traffic is awful. Nothing's moving, it's beyond gridlock, you're freezing because your car heater works only when the car is actually going someplace, which it's not—so you start railing at the cars in front of you, telling them how to drive, which of course does no good, and you're just beside yourself by the time you do get home. Which is a zoo. The house is a mess, the kids haven't touched their homework, your spouse looks up bleary-eyed at you from the couch where he's trying to take a nap (a nap, how dare he!), and dinner hasn't even been considered, much less started. You explode: "Is it too much to ask to have a halfway cleaned-up house, homework done routinely, and dinner started by 6:30 P.M.?" You shout orders to everyone in sight and then storm off to your bedroom, furious, slamming the door hard behind you.

And tomorrow is the same story. It seems that no matter how hard you try to get your family to do things the way you want them to, it never sticks, just as no matter how loudly you tell other drivers how they should drive, it never works.

What's wrong? What's going on here? *When we can't control our environment, we try to control people.* Controlling people never works. It's as simple as that. Umpteen rebellions, revolutions, uprisings, and homicides have resulted from people trying to control people. Short-term, it often seems like a workable solution. Long-term, it always fails. What does work? Cooperating with people, negotiating with people, understanding people, and working with them—that works. The problem is that cooperating and working with others to get what you want takes a willingness many of us lack.

"Hey, I'm willing," you say, "other people just don't want to do things the right way." What you mean by "the right way," however, is—your way. Wanting things done your way is just another word for controlling people. The willingness I am talking about is the willingness to give up the idea that your way is "the right way" and instead, open up to the idea that there are many "right ways" to get things done. Usually, as many as there are people involved!

"Great," you groan, "I can just see it now: The kids' idea of how to get dinner on is to order pizza, and my spouse's idea of a clean house is a clear lane to the TV. I can't live that way!" No, of course you can't, and that's not what "working with" others is about. The idea is not for each to do individually what he or she thinks is "the right thing," but for all the people involved to agree on a common goal and then figure out how best to reach that goal given their individual talents and preferences.

For example, let's say you sit down with your family and agree that a common goal is a clean house. A clean house is more pleasant to live in, smells better, and everybody can find his or her "stuff" more easily. Fine. So far, so good. As the main clean-obsessed parent, you draw up a list of what you think it takes to keep a house clean. Then you pass the list around the table and see who agrees/disagrees with the elements of a clean house. Your family agrees with most of the items on your list, they just think less frequency is better. OK. You compromise. Floors will get washed once a week, not every day.

Now comes the part you dread. Who will do which item? Ask! Don't impose, ask (there's a novel idea): "Who wants to take which item? We have to accomplish all of them, so choose." You each pick one item from the list and keep passing the list around until all items are chosen. Each week a different family member is in charge of supervising that everything is done OK. Everybody gets to clean the way he or she wants to as long as the finished product meets the "supervisor's" approval. That means your preteen daughter gets to listen to her Walkman while vacuuming, and your teen-aged son can talk on the phone while doing dishes. No, things won't get done "your way"—but they'll get done, and you'll find that your home (your "environment") comes gently under control, even as you no longer control the people in it.

Ah, the paradoxes of life . . .

One *of the best ways to persuade others is with* *your ears—by listening to them.*

DEAN RUSK

The Curse of
Runaway Emotions

When you're in the grip of a strong emotion, it feels as if that's all you are, that you are just one seething mass of anger or a giant blob of sadness or a great empty yawning hole of loneliness. But, in fact, you are none of these things. You are—you. And you are a complex being, who, among other things, feels emotions. You are not your emotions, any more than you are your mind or your appetite or your muscles. Letting any one part of you run the whole show is bound to get you into trouble.

You're angry at your mate, let's say, because for the umpteenth time he left the bathroom an absolute mess. You say to yourself as you stomp around picking things up: "I'm so angry—he knows perfectly well I hate messes, boy, am I mad!" Now, up to here, everything's fine: Your emotions are letting you know how you feel about the situation, and that is precisely what emotions are supposed to do. The problem for most of us, though, is that we don't stop there and respond to the emotion by figuring out an appropriate course of action; instead, we react to the emotion itself and let our anger generate more anger.

"I'm angry at my mate for not picking up the bathroom" becomes "What a jerk he is, he can never do anything right, I just hate the way he . . ." and we're off and running. We let the initial anger trigger more anger and it starts to snowball: We go on to being angry at our mate for all sorts of things completely unrelated to the bathroom mess and then go on to finding a zillion things to be angry about regarding our life in general.

Don't become your emotions. Instead, be aware of them and then respond appropriately. Use your mind to figure out what is the most appropriate response to your feelings, given the situation. That's what minds are for, figuring things out, and they do that very well. Sometimes the most appropriate thing to do is simply to vent your feelings in a safe way (for example, put a pillow in the middle of your bed and punch it); sometimes it's to verbally confront the person who has triggered your feelings in an assertive (not aggressive!) fashion; sometimes it's to acknowledge the emotion as a warning signal—without venting it or expressing the feeling directly—and simply going on to a problem-solving phase, and so on. Whatever response you choose, you will be allowing your emotions to fulfill their duty to you (letting you know how you feel about what is going on), and you will not be MIS-USING your emotions, which is what you do when you let them take over and be everything.

You are not your emotions. You are much more than that. Your emotions flow through you much as water flows through a riverbed. When you notice you're feeling something troubling, stop for a moment, observe the emotion, "I'm feeling sad, I'm disappointed," and ask yourself "What is this telling me? What do I need to do to get myself to a happy place?" Then use your excellent mind to figure out how to get you there as quickly and efficiently as possible; after all, you deserve it!

There is no duty we so much underrate as the duty of being happy.

ROBERT LOUIS STEVENSON

Fantasy Fun

You're walking along, kids in tow, trying to keep one of them from running into the street and the other one from jumping up and down in front of you every five seconds, and you see a billboard "Come to lovely Hawaii"—and the thought flashes across your mind "Oh, yes! Dump the kids/work, leave the spouse, just hop on a plane, and go sit on a sun-drenched beach drinking piña coladas and having unbelievably sexy lifeguards flirting with me," and the instant you catch yourself thinking that you start berating yourself: "How could I think that! Oh, how awful of me! I love my children, I must be a terrible parent to think such a thought, oh, my word, and I'd never cheat on my spouse, leave my work, oh, bad me, how terrible."

Well, no, not really. You didn't actually go out and dump the kids, desert the spouse, and split, did you? Of course not. What your mind just did was provide you with an escape fantasy, that's all. Unfortunately, you didn't permit yourself to enjoy it. You confused thought and feeling with behavior and reprimanded yourself for your thoughts and feelings as if you were literally going to go out and do that. Behavior is a choice. It may be an impulsive choice, but it's still a choice. Thoughts and feelings, however, come up unbidden. We can choose what we do about them, but not whether or not we're going to have them.

Use your fantasies to help you. Your fantasies, your daydreams, your dreams all exist to help you live a more expanded life than you can live in a day-to-day way in the real world. Allowing yourself to indulge in the fantasy in the preceding example, of dumping all responsibility and being pampered and flirted with, to really get into it and feel it, would refresh you, and since it's fantasy and you know you will not choose to act it out, there is no need to feel guilty or berate yourself. Knowing that just because you think something doesn't mean you have to act on it frees you.

So how can you better use your fantasies and daydreams? First, recognize they have a positive function in your life. They allow you to either work out or live out in your imagination things you would be extremely reluctant to do in real life. If, for example, you fantasize killing your boss/spouse, you're probably angry at him/her. Great! Don't shy away from that. Have a full-blown vigorous fantasy wherein you kill your boss/spouse in some wildly imaginative, satisfying way. This allows you to deal with your anger by venting it appropriately, that is to say, in a way that will not hurt anybody. If you vent it thoroughly in fantasy, you will find it relatively easy after that to drop your anger and go on to problem solving whatever brought up the anger in the first place.

Daydream deliberately. Take a ten-minute break during a stressed or harried day to imagine your favorite vacation spot, really see and hear all the sights and sounds, and let yourself feel the emotions of that special place. You will be surprised at how much more refreshed and happy you feel at the end of those ten minutes.

Stop blaming yourself for your fantasies and daydreams. Accept them for what they are, an expansion of reality, not reality itself, and enjoy!

---

*W*hen patterns are broken, new worlds can emerge.

TULI KUPFERBERG

Put the Fun Back into Your Life

When you were seven years old, you knew all about having fun. As a matter of fact, you spent most of your nonplay time trying to figure out how to get more play time. The Meaning of Life was very clear to you then: Life was there to be enjoyed, and you knew just how to do that—ride your bike, pretend to be cops and robbers, watch clouds go by, and so forth. And then, somewhere along the line, life got serious, and at about the same time, somehow life stopped being fun.

What happened? Well, quite obviously, you grew up, and with growing up came responsibilities: having to earn a living, paying bills, raising kids, and you took these responsibilities seriously, you really applied yourself to doing them "right," which is great, but in the process, you lost the art of having fun.

What is fun, anyway? Fun isn't any one thing, like going to a party or riding a roller-coaster. Fun is allowing yourself to be open and receptive to whatever can be enjoyed in any given situation at any given moment. For example, washing your car is a responsibility you take seriously, *but* you don't have to fulfill that responsibility in total seriousness. You can have fun doing it! You can enjoy the good feeling of your muscles as you wash your car or enjoy the sight and smell of the clean car when you're done.

We tend to focus so much on making things work or getting things done that we forget to enjoy them. Don't get caught up in the seriousness of it all. Yes, be responsible in your relationship, for example, and yes, work diligently at communicating better, at understanding each other better, but don't forget to have fun at it! Take the time to just plain enjoy the person you're with, to see him/her for the vibrant/quirky/passionate/mellow soul that he/she is, and enjoy that. Be willing to make having fun a priority in your life. If, for example, you don't like your job, be willing to ask yourself "OK, so what small part of my job, or of how I do my job, or of the people at my job could I possibly enjoy?" Challenge yourself to finding some enjoyable aspect, or, if you can't find one, create it. Take your lunch outside and eat it under a tree. Go to the office a half hour early and enjoy starting your day slowly without a bunch of people running around. Make having fun at whatever you do an integral part of your life.

Granted, some things leave little room for enjoyment: the death of a loved one, becoming grievously ill, but these do not constitute the majority of our lives. Most of our lives are spent in routine activities, and that's where you can create a lot more fun for yourself. Instead of focusing on how boring or difficult or painful something is, deliberately seek to have fun at it: Play your favorite music when you pay bills, put flowers on your desk at work, listen to the ball game when you do dishes. Make it a habit to factor enjoyment into everything you do and you'll be surprised at how much more fun your life is.

If a man insisted on always being serious, and never allowed himself a bit of fun and relaxation, he would go mad or become unstable without knowing it.

HERODOTUS

Growing the Love

Love is both a feeling and an action. As a feeling, it is often mysterious: Why you love the woman someone else divorced is a mystery, why you love country music when your brother hates it is equally unknowable. But the action of love, the "doing" of love is not mysterious at all, and the miracle is that as we perform the actions of loving, the feeling of love (which may or may not include "falling in love") blossoms. This is true whether we are talking about loving a person, a job, a country, or a work of art: The "doing" of love brings about the feeling of love.

What is the "doing" of love? Well, when you set out to love particular people or things you spend time with, getting to know them as they are, and you do this in a spirit of curiosity and acceptance. You recognize their way of doing things or the way they are may be unfamiliar to you, but you take these differences as interesting, not as good, bad, right, or wrong. Second, you are concerned about the particular persons' or things' well-being, you care about whether or not they are happy or well taken care of, and you take active measures to support their well-being. Third, you appreciate them. You value the persons or things you have chosen to love. You are grateful.

Gratitude can be considered the bottom line "doing" of love. If you appreciate and value certain people or things, you will automatically be concerned about their well-being and be willing to get to know and accept them. But if you don't value certain people or things, why bother?

If the quickest way to grow a love is gratitude, the reverse is also true: The quickest way to kill a love is to fail to appreciate. Our tendency, all too often, is to get caught up in the problems and difficulties and to stay stuck there, endlessly blaming, criticizing, and fault-finding. We ignore what's going right, and the love dies. So your boss complains that she has to cut costs: Now you have to log all your telephone calls, and as you moan about the new rules, you focus only on that and forget to appreciate the things you value about your job: you forget your pleasure in creating the product or how much you enjoy working with clients; you take for granted your paycheck. And the more you dwell on your unhappiness, the more flaws you find in your job, until you lose your love of it entirely.

Your spouse fails to take out the garbage, wears a shirt you hate, and falls asleep when you want to cuddle. You focus on these shortcomings and forget that this is the same person who sat by your bedside when you were sick for days on end, who loves your body even when you hate it, and who will hold you when you cry even if your spouse doesn't understand why you're crying. You focus righteously on your disappointments and forget to appreciate, to be grateful for what is good. After a while, you don't see anything to be grateful for, and the love dies. How sad!

Don't let the love die. Be grateful and express your appreciation—often, loudly, and with gusto, both to yourself and to the object of your love, and watch the love grow—and grow!

That best portion of a good man's life; his little, nameless, unremembered acts of kindness and of love.

WILLIAM WORDSWORTH

The Force of Habit

Change is difficult for most of us, yet often the only way to be happier and more satisfied in life is to make changes. You want to lose weight, you have to change your eating patterns; you want to have less stress and more energy, you have to change how you do/don't exercise; you want to get to work on time, you have to change your morning routine. Creating happier selves requires change.

Well, you're no dummy, you know that, so what's the problem? The problem is that you are starting your hundredth diet, because every time you go on a diet, you go off it within two weeks; you are joining yet another gym, too embarrassed to go back to your old gym, since you only went to it for the first ten days of your six-month membership; or after a week of valiant effort, you find yourself once again arriving late at work. You conclude you are a no-good worthless lazy substandard member of the human race, you might as well give up, what the heck, "They'd better just like me as I am," and curl up in self-pity in front of the TV with a large bag of chips.

In fact, you are not a no-good worthless lazy substandard member of the human race, you are simply not using a powerful tool you already have to help you make changes. Habit. Huh? Yes, habit. Things we do by habit are things we do virtually without thinking of them. We just do them. That is an incredibly powerful force. You put on your clothes, you eat, you even think the way you do by habit. But you didn't always have these habits. You acquired them by repeating the same behavior in the same way over and over again.

How does this relate to making changes? The easiest way to make a change in how you do things is to create a new habit, a new way of doing things automatically. How to create a new habit:

1. Tie the new habit to an old habit: An old habit is the strongest thing in the world. Use this power to your advantage. For example, you used to go home directly from work and raid the fridge. Getting into your car to go someplace (namely, home) after work is a habit. Take advantage of it by getting into your car after work (the old habit) and driving directly to the gym (the new habit you want to create).

Or, you want to get to work earlier. You like to watch the news before you go to bed. Tie a new habit (setting your clothes out the night before to shorten your morning routine) to the old habit (prebed TV watching) by getting your clothes out during the commercials.

2. Set up support and reminder mechanisms for yourself: Write reminders of the new habit you want to create and the wonderful benefits you will get from it on Post-its and stick them everywhere: in your car, on your bathroom mirror, in your appointment book, on your TV, and so on. Enlist the help of a friend: Call him daily with how you're doing, ask him to encourage you and support you when you're feeling "weak."

3. Repeat the new habit a minimum of three weeks: it takes at least three weeks for a new habit to start to take hold.

Follow #1 and #2, hang tight for those three weeks, and you'll be well on your way to the desired change and a much happier you!

You're never a loser until you quit trying.

MIKE DITKA

Don't Worry, Be Happy!

You watch the morning news: The economy is terrible, people are getting laid off, jobs are scarce, and you start to think . . . "Oh my gosh, my industry hasn't been doing so hot lately, what if they start laying people off—what if I get laid off . . . oh, that would be awful, how would I pay the rent? And my car payments, oh boy, if I couldn't pay for the car, then they'd take it away, and what am I going to do without a car? I mean I can hardly look for a job without a car, and speaking of jobs, what could I do? I've been in this industry for eight years, that's all I know and if I get laid off from here . . ." and on and on and on—you worry.

Worrying has been called the first sign of mental distress. And that's exactly what it is. When you worry, you don't just think about the same thing over and over; that might be a nuisance, but it wouldn't cause you distress. No, worrying is when you think about the same thing over and over, each time focusing on the negative aspects of the thing and each time magnifying the negative aspects of the thing—and that *does* lead to mental distress. But if someone says to you, "So, stop worrying," do you? Of course not! You don't stop worrying because you still have something to worry about. The economy is rotten, and you could get laid off. So what to do?

Well, the popular song "Don't Worry, Be Happy" has the right idea, but it's missing a piece. Really it should be called "Don't Worry; Reality Check, Problem Solve, and Be Happy" (which is accurate, but makes for a lousy song title).

Start by recognizing that your concern (getting laid off) is legitimate, but that your worry is not; your worry serves only to cause you mental anguish. Deal with your concern so that you can let go of the worry.

1. *Run a reality check.* Make an objective assessment of your industry: Has it in truth been particularly affected by the recession? Is your work realistically in danger? Assess the state of your personal finances: Do you have a savings account built up? What's the status on your bills? And so forth, objectively and realistically assessing where you are at in the area of your concern. If you don't feel you can be objective, run your reality checks by a friend.

2. *On the basis of your reality check—problem solve.* If your industry is threatened, then take advantage of this opportunity to train yourself for a type of work that is essential to the economy and therefore not likely to disappear in the near future. If your reality check shows that your job itself is safe, but you aren't doing a bang-up job, then take steps to fix that. If you don't have the cushion of a savings account, start one, and so on.

The bottom line is, as you actively take steps to problem solve, your worries will melt away. Your concern may remain, but it will no longer eat away at you and cause you distress, because you know you are handling it. Now you can truly "Don't Worry," and have the "Be Happy!" you deserve.

> *Courage is resistance to fear, mastery of fear—not absence of fear.*
>
> MARK TWAIN

The Truth, The Whole Truth

Some people seem to have no trouble saying exactly what's on their minds; they are able to express their hurt feelings or anger directly and to confront others easily and comfortably: "John, I was really hurt by what you said, and I'm angry with you for saying it." Sounds great! But for the great majority of us, expressing hurt or angry feelings, or saying something you think might hurt or anger the other person (confronting) is very difficult. You fear the other person's reaction; you're afraid of either hurting his feelings or making him angry.

The upshot is you take your feelings and try to squash them, either by minimizing them: "You know, John, um, I'm kind of a little upset, you know, by that thing you said," or by pretending they don't exist: "No, it's all right, really, I'm not angry at all," or you end up expressing your feelings inappropriately: "You horrible sickening disgusting person, how dare you say that to me!" Since none of these methods really work, you're stuck with unresolved feelings and you end up unhappy or sick or frustrated and, most certainly, in pain.

What to do? Quit holding back! Tell "the truth, the whole truth, and nothing but the truth"; in other words tell all your feelings to the person, not just the hurt or angry part.

1. *Start with exactly where you are emotionally:* "I'm nervous about talking to you about this; I'm afraid that you might get angry at me for bringing it up"; "I'm uncomfortable mentioning this; I'm concerned about your feelings, and I don't want to hurt you in any way";

"I'm scared of talking to you about this; I don't know how you feel about X, and I'm afraid you'll be mad about it"; "I'm embarrassed to bring this up; it's real difficult for me to comment on someone else's behavior, but it's important to me to try to talk about this"; "This is difficult for me to talk about, I'm not comfortable talking about personal things, but it's important for me to share it with you, even though I'm scared you may not like what you hear."

2. *Wait to see how the person responds to you.* If he says, "Well, if I get angry, I get angry, tough!" then don't continue to disclose further feelings. This is not a person open to genuine communication. Find a different way of resolving whatever the issue is. If he responds, as most people will, with something along the lines of, "Well, OK, I don't know how I'll feel about it, but I'll try to listen to you," say whatever it is you have to say. Clearly, the person still may not like what you disclose, but he is prepared to hear something potentially unpleasant and therefore is less likely to be highly reactive, and he has expressed a willingness to communicate. In this situation, you do have a good possibility of resolving the issue.

Interestingly, you take better care of yourself by putting your fears up front and owning them than you do by hiding your feelings. Shying away from difficult or painful feelings only hurts you in the end. Have the courage to state your fears, and resolving your issues becomes much easier.

---

*T*he time is always right to do what is right.

MARTIN LUTHER KING, JR.

Say "No" to Verbal Abuse

Most of us recognize physical abuse for what it is: hurtful, demeaning, and totally inappropriate. Verbal abuse is less easily recognized for what it is, emotional violence, yet it is far more common and, in its own way, doubly dangerous. Why? Because not only does verbal abuse hurt in and of itself, but verbal abuse is almost always the precursor to physical abuse. Thus learning to deal with verbal abuse in an appropriate and positive way is very important.

Verbal abuse can be simply defined as any time someone says something to you that discounts you, denies your feelings, or in some way devalues you. Discounting is failing to take into account someone else's reality: You say, "Boy, am I bushed"; she says, "You couldn't be, you didn't even come in until 10:00 today." Denial of feelings is negating how someone feels: You say, "I'm really depressed about that"; she says, "Oh, cheer up, it's really not that bad." Devaluing is treating a person in any way that takes away from his or her dignity as a human being. Name calling and/or ripping into people yelling and screaming (in the absence of an emergency situation) are devaluing.

Because verbal abuse is not so obviously hurtful as physical abuse, we often let it slip by, not realizing its cumulative damaging effects. We say to ourselves, "I'm too sensitive," or we assume that the other person must be right and we're somehow defective human beings and deserve the hurt. This is a terrible thing to do to ourselves.

Instead, deal with the abuse by drawing boundaries, setting limits, and standing up for yourself.

1. *Dealing with discounting:* You say, "Boy, am I bushed"; she says, "You couldn't be, you didn't even come in until 10:00 today." You say (drawing a boundary between your experience and her interpretation of your experience): "The time I came in today has nothing to do with my fatigue." (Now you stand up for yourself with): "I'm really tired."

2. *Dealing with denial of feelings:* You say, "I'm really depressed about that"; he says, "Oh, cheer up, it's really not that bad." You say, "Whether it's all that bad or not has nothing to do with it" (drawing a boundary between your experience and his interpretation of it—going on to stand up for yourself): "I'm really depressed about it."

When you handle discounting and denial in this way, people will generally change their approach and begin respecting your reality/feelings. However, if they persist in discounting or denying, even after you have repeated your stance once or twice, stop sharing your thoughts and feelings with these people. They don't deserve it.

3. *Dealing with devaluing:* Someone is yelling and screaming at you or calling you names, you say (standing up for yourself), "I will not be yelled at/talked to in this way" (setting clear limits). "I will listen to you/discuss this when you calm down." Then GO AWAY. Let the person know you are temporarily leaving, but LEAVE. It is not OK to let yourself be abused.

You will feel your self-esteem rise in direct proportion to how you stand up for yourself in the face of discounting, denial, and devaluing. You are a worthwhile human being—don't let anyone ever treat you as any less.

CAUTION: If you are in a situation where you fear someone might become physically abusive if you stand up for yourself, DO NOT use these techniques. Seek professional help immediately.

The fastest way to freedom is to feel your feelings.

GITA BELLIN

A Winner's Secret

When something goes wrong, it can be very satisfying to say, "Well, it's so-and-so's fault, if he'd just get with it, this wouldn't have happened," or "I know I'm late, but it's not my fault the car broke down"— and, no, it's not your fault—but, if you stop there, you've just declared yourself a loser. Yes! You've just stated that you have no power, that you are but the helpless victim of the situations and events in your life, that whatever happens, it's somebody or something else's fault, nothing you could do would matter. Not so! You have tremendous power over what happens to you *if* you stop focusing on where to fix the blame and start focusing on how to fix the situation.

This is a winner's secret. A winner has just as many difficult situations to face as anybody else, just as many unpleasant happenings and circumstances, but a winner doesn't stop at figuring out whose fault it is. A winner stops at "whose fault it is" just long enough to figure out where the responsibility lies for which portion of the problem (in order to better problem solve) and then immediately turns his or her attention to how to fix the situation: what to do to ensure that this particular situation never comes up again or what to do to remedy the situation now.

Winners are great at creative problem solving. For example, if you were late because your car broke down, maybe you need to have more regular maintenance visits to your mechanic, or maybe you need to change mechanics. Or, you might start to carry along with you the phone numbers of the appointments you are driving to, so you could call them if your car broke down again. If, for example, "so-and-so" is someone who causes you problems on the job, let's say by his lack of initiative or poor follow-through, find ways of dealing with his irresponsibility rather than simply blaming the person. Ask to work with a different individual, or don't rely on this person for initiative, don't count on his follow-through. Accept the fact that this person is unreliable and figure out creative ways to work successfully regardless of how "so-and-so" fails to do his job well.

This is what being a winner is all about—creatively using your skills and talents so that you are successful no matter what is happening around you. Winners don't have fewer problems in their lives; they are just better at seeing those problems as challenges, as opportunities to further apply, develop, and explore their own talents. Once you accept that you do have the power to transform any given situation, given your unique talents and skills, you will find that your ability to creatively problem solve is tremendous.

So, stop focusing on "whose fault it is." Who cares! Start focusing on the wonderful opportunity of applying your strengths and talents to problem solve, and use whatever happens to you in your life as just another stepping stone to a better, happier life.

Man, unlike any other thing organic or inorganic in the universe, grows beyond his work, walks up the stairs of his concepts, emerges ahead of his accomplishments.

JOHN STEINBECK

How to Make Worry
Your Friend(!)

The idea of worry as being anything even remotely "friendly" may seem absurd, yet every emotion has both its positive and negative function. Unfortunately, we usually see only the negative side of worry, which is to make us increasingly anxious about everything.

Here is an example: "The traffic is awful, what if I don't get there in time, I'll bet my dress/suit is going to be just a wrinkled mess from sitting in here, they're going to think I'm totally unprofessional, I'll never get this job . . ." "What if I can't find a relationship, I'll be lonely and miserable forever . . ." "What if I don't hear the alarm and I sleep through this interview . . ." "What if I go to the party and I don't know anyone there and I'll feel so stupid and I won't know what to say . . . ," and it goes on and on. We worry about everything from the vitally important to the clearly absurd.

The problem is, we're not using worry to its best advantage. Worry does have a positive function, a beautiful and wonderful function—it is a warning signal, an internal feedback mechanism that tells us "Hey, pay attention, there may be some danger here." Used properly, worry is valuable.

So, how do you use worry properly? Heed the warning! Let worry be your friend, alerting you to potential problems, and figure out possible solutions before you go into the situation.

For example, think before you go off to that important meeting: Is the traffic likely to be bad? Should you consider an alternate, perhaps longer, but less hassled route? If you are likely to be in the car a long time, choose clothes that won't wrinkle, or remember to hang your jacket in the back. If, despite all your good efforts, you are late, have you thought of the best, most professional way to present your lateness?

For example, if you are worried you'll end up alone and unhappy, learn about how to create a satisfying relationship, put yourself out there, take the necessary steps. If you are concerned about sleeping through your alarm on an important day, set two/three/four alarms, ask a friend to call you, rather than simply worry yourself to death over it. If you are worried about not knowing anyone at a social event, figure out topics of conversation that are of common interest and decide that this is a great opportunity to make new friends. If you are worrying about something for which you can't figure out solutions on your own, ask for help. Ask as many people as you need to, then sort through their different ideas and choose the one that feels best to you.

Once you have figured out practical, workable solutions to your worries, drop them. Just let them go. If the same worries drift through your mind, remind yourself: "I already dealt with that," and if they keep drifting through, then use an imaginary fist of white light to !POW! those worries right out of your mind. Hanging on to worries you've thought through is the mental equivalent of letting the alarm clock ring once you're up . . . annoying and useless.

Worry is a great friend when you need it, but a big drag when you're just carting it along for the ride.

> *The reason why worry kills more people than work is that more people worry than work.*
>
> ROBERT FROST

What's Wrong
With Me/Them?

Nothing is going right. You turn in a report, your boss criticizes it mercilessly; you try to have a "civilized" discussion with your ten-year-old, he turns into a three-year-old tantruming baby; you try to get the mechanic to rerepair the whatever on your car that still isn't working right, and he treats you like a complete fool for even asking, and you end up yelling at the top of your lungs (out loud or inside yourself) one of two things *"What's wrong with me?"* or *"What's wrong with them?"*

Your frustration is totally understandable, but your conclusion, that somehow something must be wrong with you/them, is not helpful. You are not a broken machine, needing to be fixed. Nor are they. What you and/or they are is a person lacking in certain skills, in need of different ways of coping and responding to life's events. You, however, are the only one you can change. So that's where you start, with yourself. The question becomes not "What's wrong with me/them?" but "How can I approach this situation differently? What skills or ways of responding can I use here that would be more successful?"

For example, when your boss criticizes your report mercilessly, try to find out how you can do it better next time: "I understand you don't like how I researched this; what do you see as better ways for me to do the research?" "I understand you don't like how I pulled the material together, how would you like me to do it?" If your boss doesn't have a helpful answer (it happens—many people are much better at criticizing than they are at constructive comments), then ask him to give you an example of a report researched and written in a way that works for your boss. Then figure out for yourself how that report differs from yours. Get help. Ask colleagues/friends who have similar tasks how they go about it. Keep looking for answers to the question, "How can I make this work for me?" rather than "What's wrong with me/them?"

Similarly, in communicating with your child/the mechanic, seek out communication techniques that will allow you to interact more successfully. For example, with your child, use periods of "time out" when your child resorts to tantrums instead of conversation. Teach your child (by role modeling as well as by instructing) how to first listen to what the other person has to say, clarify ("OK, so what you're telling me is you want me to X . . ."), and then respond.

Communication may be a natural impulse, but successful communication is a learned skill, as is true of most things in life. In order to communicate successfully with your mechanic, try out techniques such as "broken record," where you clearly identify your need and repeat it over and over again: "I understand you already repaired it, but it's not working and I want it repaired again," "I understand what you're telling me, but it's not working and I want it repaired again," and so on.

Switching your focus from blaming self/others to learning skills is exciting and empowering. It goes a long way toward helping you have the successful and happy life you deserve.

In the middle of difficulty lies opportunity.

ALBERT EINSTEIN

Don't Let Fear
Run the Show!

Fear is a survival mechanism. Fear is an important contributor to your daily well-being. Fear keeps you safe. Fear is an automatic (sometimes learned, sometimes instinctive) response to anything your subconscious thinks might harm you: someone driving too fast, someone coming at you angrily, someone yelling at you. Because fear is automatic, it happens very fast. You don't sense yourself actively thinking, "Oh my gosh, that person is yelling at me, they may have it in for me in a big way, they may punch my lights out next," even though that is exactly what is happening inside you. The thought happens so fast you just know "I'm scared."

Now this is great when you're faced with imminent physical threat; after all, who wants to sit around and think about it for five minutes when a speeding car is about to ram you into never-never land. Fear, in that type of situation, is truly your friend. The problem is, fear doesn't necessarily do a good job of discriminating what genuinely is a threat to your well-being; and what is simply something unfamiliar. Fear, in its overriding desire to keep you safe, defines anything that is unfamiliar—as threatening. And that is what keeps many of us from achieving the happiness and success we long for. Fear of the unfamiliar.

For example: You hate your job. You thought you signed on for a creative, challenging career, and instead find that all you do is shuffle papers and rehash the higher-ups' ideas. You're bored, angry, and frustrated, and this has been going on for three years now. Your friends, family, and loved ones are all sick to death of hearing you complain about your job. "Why don't you quit?!" they exclaim, and you come up with numerous "good" reasons why you don't quit, all of which could be summed up in two words, "I'm scared." Scared of not really knowing what you want, scared of knowing what you want and its being unobtainable, scared of the "state of the economy," scared of trading in a "sure thing" for an unsure thing, and the list goes on. But the bottom line is—you're scared of the unfamiliar.

Fear is what makes you reason this way: "Better I should stick with a lousy but familiar situation than risk venturing into an unfamiliar situation." Fear doesn't stop and think, "Gee, maybe this unfamiliar situation could be a good situation." That's not in fear's repertoire. Fear doesn't reason things out. Fear simply responds in predictable, safety-oriented ways. Thinking is your job. And that's the good news.

Thinking is something we all can do—some better than others, no doubt, but everybody (barring disastrous brain damage) can think. Thinking through your fear is what will let fear serve you as a valuable warning device without standing in the way of your success. Think for yourself. Don't let fear do your thinking for you. When you get scared, *and there's no immediate physical threat,* ask yourself: "What am I scared of here?" And *think your way through your fears.*

In the preceding example, one of the fears was: "I'm scared of not really knowing what I want." OK, so ask yourself, "How could I look at what I might want; what tools or resources do I have to help me look at what I might want?" Another was, "I'm scared that what I want to do is unobtainable." That's understandable, so acknowledge that you're scared but then, *think,* "Well how true is that? Is what I want truly unobtainable? How close can I get to what I want? Would that make me happy? What have other people done in similar circumstances? Whom could I ask about this?"

The more you are willing to be aware of your fear, yet not let it stand in the way of your exploring unfamiliar territory, the better your chances of making that unfamiliar territory familiar and thus no longer frightening. The scary thing in the closet is no longer scary once the lights are on, and you can see what's in the closet. And if the "thing" in the closet is still frightening, at least now you can deal with the "thing" itself, rather than just being overwhelmed by the fear.

Make fear a servant, not a master. Don't let fear run the show. Use the wonderful gift of your mind, and *think* your way past fear into the success you deserve.

> *We are what we think. All that we are arises with our thoughts. With our thoughts, we make our world.*
>
> BUDDHA

The Power of Expectation

Your last three relationships have been awful. Somehow you always find yourself in relationship hell. This last one was the definitive bummer. Your girlfriend turned out to be unbelievably self-centered, demanding, controlling. When you finally got out of the relationship, heart bruised and soul battered, you felt as if you had barely escaped with your emotional life, and you have lived like a hermit ever since.

Friends are appalled: "You can't stay in your cave forever!" they cry. "Oh, yes I can," you say. "It's just fine in here. Besides, there's no one out there for me. All the good ones are either of the wrong sexual persuasion or taken, and even if I found someone 'right' for me, clearly I can't 'do' relationship, I just proved that beyond all doubt." But friends insist, family won't leave you alone, so just to keep them all quiet, you give in: "All right, I'll . . . (you swallow hard) . . . DATE. I'll try—OK?" And off you go, into the wild blue yonder of dating, and what do you find? Lo and behold, all the good ones are of the wrong sexual persuasion and/or taken, which ends the whole question of relationship right there, nah!

No, what it ends is any possibility of a good relationship *given your present belief system*. You see, what you believe is going to happen impacts what you expect is going to happen. And what you expect is going to happen influences what *does* happen in your reality. Scientists have proven this over and over: If scientist *A* expects outcome *A* from a given experiment, then *A* is likely to happen. If scientist *B* expects outcome *B* from the same experiment, then B is likely to happen. Same experiment, different expectations of outcome, *different outcomes!* The reasons for this are too long to go into here; for now, realize that *what you expect largely determines what you get.* If you expect not to find a suitable partner for relationship, you won't find one. You either won't notice the suitable ones who fall across your path, or you will dismiss potentially suitable partners for all sorts of "good" reasons.

When you're not getting something you want in your life, look to your expectations. Ask yourself: "What do I really expect in this situation?" Not what you tell everybody else you expect, not what you superficially tell yourself, but what you deep down, really expect. If what you really expect is that you won't find someone to love, then you won't find anyone. It doesn't matter how hard you try, it won't happen. However, if you change your expectations so that you genuinely expect to find such a person, then you do have a chance.

Changing your expectations takes more than positive thinking: "OK, now I expect to find a love." To truly change your expectations, change the belief system underlying your expectations.

1. *Take stock of your beliefs.* Your beliefs about something are what fuel your expectations about that something. If, for example, you believe that you are not worth much, that nobody could really love someone like you, then your expectations will reflect that belief.

2. *Change your beliefs.* Once you've uncovered your lack of self-worth, for example, work with yourself on changing it. There are wonderful tools available to you: cognitive restructuring, meditation, visualizations, to name but a few. Get a good self-help book on self-worth, and/or work with a counselor, a support group.

3. *Affirm and practice living according to your new beliefs.* Use affirmations to reinforce and support the changes you're making in #2. Practice living your new beliefs by, for example, asking yourself, "How

would a person with strong positive self-worth behave in this situation?" and as best you can, behave that way yourself.

4. *Reshape your expectations according to your new beliefs:* "OK, I really feel now that I am a worthy human being. I expect to be able to find someone who wants to interact with a worthy person and can treat me as such."

5. *Look for experiences to match your new expectations.* We really do find what we're looking for. Your new expectations will unerringly guide you to new experiences that support those expectations. Even as you still sometimes find yourself drawn to situations reflecting your old expectations, more and more you'll find yourself encountering a new and different reality. Allow it in! And enjoy.

Seek and ye shall find.

MATTHEW 7:7

Winner in the Making

There are times when it really all seems too much: when a divorce shatters a marriage you thought would last forever; when the company you've worked for for 20 years "downsizes," and suddenly you're expendable; when the child who is the light of your life is struck with an incurable disease. You cry, rant, rave, you lash out at God, the Universe, mankind, the Fates, and feel crushed, defeated, a victim, at a loss . . .

"What's wrong with me? Why couldn't I keep my marriage together, what a bad, horrible person I am . . . I don't deserve to be loved." "How could they do this to me? I've been a loyal employee there for 20 years—and this is my reward?" "How could this happen? How could my child be so ill? Why can't they find a cure? They don't care! The whole medical establishment doesn't care!"

And for a time, such feelings are normal and healthy. You are angry, frustrated, hurt, and torn apart. You have suffered horrible damage: It is tragic, it is awful. Venting such feelings in a support group, with friends, with a counselor, into a journal, is an important part of healing. The problem lies not in having those feelings or in venting them, the problem occurs when you're unwilling to let go of the pain once you've truly acknowledged and expressed it, when you use the pain to redefine yourself either as a victim or as a totally "bad/wrong" human being. If you define yourself as a victim, you'll seek to blame your world for victimizing you. If you define yourself as "bad/wrong," you'll blame yourself for all the ills that befall you. Either position is defeatist and drains you of your power.

Don't sabotage your life with such erroneous self- or world-images. As difficult as such tragedies are to deal with when they happen, in the long run such events are critical turning points, opportunities for major growth. This is not to say that you have to have such tragedies in order to grow—*absolutely not,* but to say that *if* you do have such tragedies, use them as springboards to growth rather than as excuses to turn yourself into a permanent victim.

"But it is horrible and I feel awful." Of course you do. So that's where you start, with your feelings.

1. *Feel your feelings, express them, release them.* The more willing you are to really feel all your feelings regarding the situation, the more quickly and fully you'll be able to genuinely release them. Get help in doing this. It can feel very scary to try to deal with feelings of this magnitude by yourself.

2. *Look for the lessons.* Once you've dealt with your feelings, you're ready to look at the lessons implicit in the situation. Don't dwell on blaming yourself or others, look for what *understandings* you can glean from the tragedy to help you thrive in the future. With the failed marriage, for example, did you choose an appropriate partner to start with, or did you allow your low self-esteem to choose whoever might give you even a little love as a life mate? Did you ignore all signs of trouble in the relationship until it was too late? What can you learn from this? How can you use the failed marriage to springboard you to future relationship success? With the downsizing: Did you ignore the writing on the wall? Did you take your job for granted and cease to find ways to continuously make yourself valuable to the company? What can you use here to help you for the next job? With your ailing child: What reserves of strength and love do you have you didn't even know about? What have you learned about the importance of loving and car-

ing? Can you apply those lessons to creating a support group for parents of similarly ill children, or for lobbying for a bill to get help, or for raising funds for new medical research? All of these are *empowering* questions that seek to use the disasters of the past to create a better, happier future.

3. *Be kind to yourself.* Recognize you've been through a lot. If you dump into self-pity or blame from time to time, learn to spot it, try not to run on it for too long, but don't beat yourself up for it. You're too good and too valuable a human being to do that.

Caterpillars turn to mush inside their cocoons on their way to becoming butterflies. When tragedy strikes and you turn to mush, remember, you are always a winner in the making; all it takes is the willingness to let go—and fly.

Experience is not what happens to a man; it is what a man does with what happens to him.

ALDOUS HUXLEY

Rocking the Boat (Safely)

Things are OK in your life. You have an OK job with an OK boss, you have an OK apartment with an OK landlord. You have an OK relationship with your significant other, you feel OK about yourself. Not fantastic, nothing to write home about, but OK. Meaning—well, meaning—boring, stuck, ho-hum, joyless, routine. You feel as if all you do is go through the motions, and you begin to wonder: "Is this all there is?" "Is this what it's all about?"

And then you (mentally) slap yourself upside the head and say, "Hey, shape up! Some people don't have jobs at all, or homes, or relationships, or a halfway sense of self, so what the heck, I should just be quiet and not rock my boat. Things are OK." Then you wonder, six months down the line, why you find it so hard to get out of bed in the morning, and when did veging in front of the TV become so attractive?

You're stuck. There's a fancy clinical diagnosis for you—stuck. When people stop reaching and stretching and growing, they get stuck. Just like your car: If you don't put your foot on the gas pedal, nothing happens. The motor is running, everything is in place, but the car isn't going anywhere. It's OK, not a bad thing, but certainly doesn't provide the fun or possibilities that come once you put your foot to the gas pedal. So, too, when people are stuck; it's not a bad thing, but it sure doesn't measure up to what life is and can be all about.

"But why rock the boat?" you ask. "What guarantee do I have that if I do try to get things 'unstuck' they will be better? Maybe they'll only get worse! Then where would I be—unstuck all right, and miserable!" An understandable fear, no doubt. It's certainly a possibility, one that keeps many people from growing. But it's a *false* fear, for there are many ways to grow safely and joyously. All you have to do is go about your growth in a conscious and deliberately constructive way.

1. *Dream your dreams.* Decide what would contribute to greater joy in your life (the true definition of growth): a deeper love with your significant other, a nicer apartment, a more rewarding job? Daydream, fantasize, visualize what that would be like. Then sit down, with paper and pen, and figure out what would be the likely steps to allowing that dream to happen.

2. *Do your research.* Do you have the necessary information, skills, and tools to enable you to accomplish your first step? For example, if your dream is a more rewarding job, first you have to figure out what that might be. "More rewarding" certainly implies not only a job that would fulfill your heart and soul, but also one that would afford you a better lifestyle, a more joyous and supportive work environment, bring you coworkers and bosses who enjoy working together and are appreciative of your input, and so on. Take the time and effort to figure out the specifics of what that job might be, what it would look like.

3. *Take small steps.* The easiest way not to scare yourself half to death is to take small steps to growth. It's just like putting your foot on the gas pedal. If you slam your foot down and floor the pedal, you'll go zooming off at a speed that makes crashing into something highly likely. If you gently give a little gas to the pedal, you'll start going forward without terrifying or endangering yourself. So perhaps the first step in creating a more rewarding job for yourself would be to learn a new skill, or upgrade an old one. Take small steps! Larger ones will become more comfortable as you succeed with the smaller steps.

4. *Keep moving.* Evaluate your progress, make whatever changes are appropriate, and take another small step. The secret to growth is to keep moving. Many people find it helpful to give themselves deadlines: "I'll learn the new computer program by January," for example. You'd be amazed at how much growth can be accomplished one small step at a time.

Being "stuck" is equivalent to slow death. We were not meant to stand in place. Life is full and rich and just waiting for you to enjoy it to the hilt. Take the risk of rocking your "OK" boat in a safe manner, and give yourself the joy of reaching, stretching, and growing into the happiness, success, and love you truly deserve.

> W*e lift ourselves by our thought, we climb upon our vision of ourselves.*
>
> ORISON SWEET MARDEN

When "It's to Die For" = Dead

"**O**h, it's to die for," you say of a wonderful experience.

"I just love her to death," your friend says of his new flame.

"He gives me a pain in the neck!" you say in exasperation.

"No pain, no gain," you groan as you work into the wee hours of the night. "No rest for the weary."

"It's too easy," you say of a happiness that just dropped into your life, "it's incredible!"

And your subconscious, which is programmed on a daily basis by the thoughts and beliefs you repeat continuously to yourself, strives valiantly to give you what you want. So that wonderful experience you would "die for" becomes unattainable or rare (since you hold other beliefs that say "I want to live"), your friend's new love walks out on him, feeling imprisoned and suffocated. You do, indeed, develop a stiffness in your neck, and it's remarkable just how much struggle and suffering seems to go into your every tiny advancement . . .

I could go on and on, with examples of how your subconscious devotedly translates your words into your experience of life. Words are powerful. Let me repeat that: *Words are POWERFUL.* Words are *symbols for experience.* Your subconscious mind takes those symbols and attempts to make your experience of life conform to what you keep saying to yourself. After all, if you always say "It's too easy" to yourself when anything comes your way without struggle or hardship, it only makes sense that your subconscious would figure, "Oh, OK, so she doesn't like it when things come easily. No problem, I'll help her find lots of problems and stumbling blocks to any good thing. That way it will come 'hard' and he will be happy."

Your subconscious takes you literally. That's one of the reasons people who tend to see life in a positive way live a happier life. They have programmed their subconscious (without realizing they were doing it) to seek out the positive side of experiences and make those readily available. The person who, on the other hand, holds the belief (and thoughts that go with it) "Life's a bitch and then you die" is likely to experience life in exactly those terms.

"I got it," you say, "I'll just say 'I'm happy, I'm happy, I'm happy' all the time and my subconscious will start bringing me happy experiences." Well, yes and no. If you say "I'm happy, this is great" to yourself when you get a cold, your subconscious will pair the two and promptly provide you with lots of colds because that is what makes you happy. Not a good idea. The more useful answer is *become more conscious of what you are saying to yourself about any experience and shape your thoughts and beliefs to match the experience you genuinely want.*

If you get a cold, for example, say to yourself: "This is not fun. I do not like being sick. I like health. I love being healthy. I can feel the health in my little toe right now (given that your little toe isn't feeling weak and sneezy), and I like that. I look forward to good health!" Now that's lining up what you tell your subconscious with what is real for you.

If you say to yourself: "I'm a wimp. I'm totally untrustworthy. I just go around and break my word all the time. I'm a terrible person," your subconscious will figure that's what you want your experience of life to be. After all, you keep repeating it to yourself. Your subconscious doesn't read that statement as your being in your self-pity mode, it thinks this is your truth, how you perceive yourself and want to be perceived. Be real. Suit your words to your desired experience. "OK, so I messed up—more than once. But I am not a terrible person, I want to be trustworthy and true. I am willing to be trustworthy and true. I am becoming more trustworthy and true every day." And as you affirm this to yourself, your subconscious will pick up the drift and start to steer you in that direction. As you consciously make an effort to *live* in this more trustworthy way, you reinforce that belief and those thoughts, strengthening your new subconscious programming.

Life is an art, and its primary tool is being conscious. The more you become aware of your participation in the forces that shape your life, the more you can direct your life in ways that make you happy. Then the cry no longer becomes "It's too good to be true," but *"It's good enough to be true!"*

---

*T*wixt the optimist and pessimist, the difference is droll: The optimist sees the doughnut, the pessimist sees the hole.

MCLANDBURGH WILSON

Listening with Your Heart

Your friend is upset with you. "I want to talk with you," she says. "I'm really upset over how you rushed me through the mall the other day—" and before your friend even finishes her sentence, you're apologizing: "Yes, I know, I'm sorry, I realized later it wasn't a nice thing to do but I was so worried about getting home to the kids, what could I do?" And you're on to the next thing.

Later, your coworker asks you why you left a project unfinished and you say, "Oh, well I thought it would be better if I ran it by so-and-so before going on with the revisions." He replies, "You could have told me what you were up to," and immediately you say, "I know, I should have, but I was overloaded and trying to do everything at once, and I was doing the best I could." And you're off and running.

You don't understand why your coworker is cool to you the next day, nor why, in general, people seem less willing to hang out with you. You know you take responsibility for the things you do that inconvenience or hurt people, so what's going on? Aren't apologies good enough? Do people just love to hold grudges?

Well, the truth is, apologies aren't good enough. Apologies are only as good as the behavioral changes that follow them. And it's less that people love to hold grudges, more that people hold on to their hurt until it has been expressed and resolved or healed.

"Great," you say, "so when did I become shrink to the world? I have enough on my plate already!" It's not about become "shrink to the world." It's about giving people the space to express themselves enough and in a way that allows them to *feel truly heard.*

There is a world of difference between listening with your ears and listening with your heart in a way that makes the other person feel heard. We live in hurried times, where so much emphasis is put on deadlines and schedules that too little time is accorded to the human need for expression. Yet listening with your heart doesn't take much time, and it makes a tremendous difference in the quality of all your relationships.

So how do you listen with your heart?

1. *Don't start off by apologizing.* "Huh?" you say, completely confused, "I thought apologizing if you did something hurtful was the right thing to do!" It is, but it's not the right place to *start.* The right place to start is by listening.

2. *Stop whatever you are doing and really listen to the person.* Listen with your eyes as well as your ears. Look at the person as he is telling you how he feels about the way you hurt or inconvenienced him. Don't fidget, watch TV, or file your nails at the same time. Give him your complete and undivided attention.

3. *Resist the temptation to defend yourself.* This is a hard one for most of us. You like to think of yourself as a good person and when you've hurt someone, it's usually not deliberate. So there's a natural tendency to jump in with your explanations, excuses, defenses, and rationalizations. Resist, resist, resist.

4. *Acknowledge what the person feels.* "It was really uncomfortable for you to be rushed like that," "You felt really ignored, as if I wasn't paying any attention to your needs," "It felt as if I didn't value your opinion" are all examples of acknowledging what a person says to you about his feelings.

5. *Be courageous enough to ask (genuinely), "Is there anything else?"* "Ouch!" you say, "that could really hurt!" Certainly, if you haven't been truly listening to your friend for a long time, it could hurt, there might be piles and piles of resentful feelings built up. If, however, you listen to people as soon as something comes up, there won't be much "else." And it is important that the person have the opportunity to really speak her piece.

6. *Apologize.* Now is the time to apologize, graciously and honestly. You still don't need to defend or justify. The apology is sufficient.

7. *Make amends and/or change your future behavior.* An apology has no value unless it is backed up with action. Amends are often the most powerful way to apologize.

This whole process can take less than five minutes yet make the difference between a thriving relationship and a stultifying one. Give yourself the benefit of being who you truly are: one who listens, one who cares, one who *hears*.

Life shrinks or expands in proportion to one's courage.

ANAÏS NIN

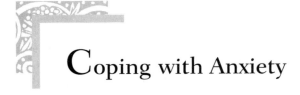

Coping with Anxiety

Your heart suddenly starts pounding, you can't seem to breathe or catch your breath, you have no idea what's going on, you think you're losing your mind, you're scared to death—welcome to the overwhelming world of panic attacks . . .

Anxiety seems to be one of the primary disorders of our times. It doesn't seem to matter whether you're rich or poor, doing well or doing badly, in good health or ill; at some point, most of us experience that awful form of anxiety known as a "panic attack."

One of the most difficult things about panic attacks is that they seem to come "out of the blue," for no apparent reason. There you are, tooling along, things seem to be going along just fine or no worse or differently than usual, when WHAM—it hits. That is what makes "panic attacks" so crazy making. Your house hasn't burned down, you're not in the middle of an earthquake, your child hasn't vanished . . . so why are you feeling this way?

Anxiety might be thought of as the "what if" disorder: *"What if* my house burns down, I get cancer and I can't work anymore, my job is downsized, I get older and nobody wants me, my child gets kidnapped by some crazy person . . ." and on and on. When the "what ifs" start, if left to grow unchecked, they can easily grow into a full-blown panic attack.

Your body and your mind are connected. I know this sounds simplistic, but we often forget that what we think and how we feel directly impacts our bodies. When the "what ifs" start and are allowed to keep coming unanswered, your body gets ready for disaster. As you raise your emotional fear level, your body responds by getting ready either to fight or flee (the two basic survival reactions) by pumping adrenaline like crazy into your body systems. Since you don't go anywhere, there you are with all that essentially unused adrenaline flowing through your bloodstream, revving up your body systems, making your heart thud, ruining your digestive system, and generally making you SURE you are having a heart attack.

So what to do? Well, first of all, see a medical doctor and make sure that your heart really is OK and that the rest of you is functioning normally. When the doctor reassures you that, yes, you are fine, you're "just anxious," resist the impulse to tell the doctor she is out of her mind, that obviously you are having a heart attack. If your doctor prescribes antianxiety medication, take it. When the medication makes you feel fine, don't assume that "Oh, I just needed some medicine." NO! The antianxiety medication causes your symptoms to subside, but it doesn't deal with what's really going on, what is causing the anxiety in the first place. So have the courage to deal with your anxiety directly.

Put down on paper all the fears you are having, the "what ifs" that are running nonstop through your mind. Look at each one, one at a time, perhaps only one or two per day, and take the fear apart. For example, you fear your job is going to disappear. OK, how realistic a fear is that? If this particular job does disappear, are you prepared to take your skills elsewhere? Would it be wise to get some additional training or learn some new skills at this time? Is this actually a blessed opportunity to get into something you'd really like to do? Anxiety melts as you deal realistically with your fear. Once you have sorted out what you can do, take action! There is nothing quite so empowering as taking action. One step at a time is quite sufficient; just keep moving in the desired direction.

Anxiety can be a real joy killer. Be willing to answer the "what ifs" with creative problem solving and take your life back. The more quickly and thoroughly you deal with your underlying fears, the more anxiety can serve the purpose it was originally intended for—a warning, not the monster that runs your life.

> *In the darkest hour the soul is replenished and given strength to continue and endure.*
>
> HEART WARRIOR CHOSA

The Power of Choice

You are having lunch with your coworkers. You are in the midst of a heated discussion, everyone joining in, giving ideas. You give your opinion and one of your coworkers replies, "Oh, that's ridiculous! How in the world can you think that" and you shrivel up inside, devastated by her retort. You feel your face getting all hot and flushed, you'd like to slink under the table and crawl out of the cafeteria unnoticed . . .

You're helping a friend work on a project. It's not going well, there's a deadline, and your friend is getting increasingly frustrated. Finally he just blows up, saying, "You're not helping! You're only making it worse! I should never have asked you to help—now I'm really confused and you've made it horribly complicated, and I'm going to be even more over my deadline . . . ," and on and on. You're stunned—and you promptly blow up in return. "Well, if that's how you feel about it, see if I help you again!" and out the door you storm, stomping your feet and slamming the door for good measure.

What just happened? Why did you react so strongly? Nothing earthshaking happened, nothing life threatening, so why are you either feeling devastated and lower than an earthworm, or fuming, ready to punch something?

Your feelings were hurt, that much is obvious. And hurt is a normal, natural reaction to someone putting down your opinion or failing to value your input. However, as natural and instinctive as the reaction may be, your response to your hurt—either to devalue yourself or blow up at the other—is not instinctive, it is chosen.

"Huh?" you ask. "Chosen? How can I choose something like that—it just happens!" No, it doesn't. Even if there is only a nanosecond between the hurt you feel and your response to that hurt, there is time in there during which you do, albeit usually on a subconscious level, choose your response.

That puts you in the power seat! That is good news. You see, anytime you are at choice with something, you have power. It's when people feel they don't have choice that you feel powerless. "OK, fine," you say, not real happy about the idea, but accepting it, "so what am I supposed to choose in that nanosecond, and how?"

1. *Stop.* When you feel yourself reacting strongly to something with either hurt or anger, stop. Take a moment to breathe, which will help you settle down inside yourself.

2. *You are worthy.* Remind yourself that you are a good and worthy person, that whatever is going on doesn't change that. Regardless of what your ideas, opinions, and ways of doing things are, they are yours, and as such are valuable.

3. *Don't accept the hurt.* Just because someone says something that hurts or angers you doesn't mean you have to respond in a hurt or angry mode. You can choose to respond differently.

4. *Seek to understand.* Now, rather than go into self-destruct or other-destruct, go into an understanding mode. As best you can, try to understand what is going on with the other person. You can do that either by directly asking her: "I'm curious, what makes you say that?" "I'm confused—can you clarify for me what you mean by that?" or, to go back to our original example: "Well, clearly I do think this way—what is it about my opinion that you find 'ridiculous'?"

With your frustrated friend, it may not be timely to ask questions; he is possibly too frustrated to answer appropriately. You can, however, recognize that your friend is blowing up out of his frustration at the situation and empathize with that. Be quiet for a moment. Then respect your friend's need for space by leaving, but also support him by letting him know you're there for him if he needs you. "OK, I know it's really frustrating for you. I'm sorry I couldn't be of more help. I'll be at home if you need me."

Most of the pokes and jabs we feel in the course of an ordinary day aren't meant to hurt us, they are the result of someone's aggravation with something else, or of his or her failure to say things in ways that respect people's feelings. The more you are able and willing to understand why people are saying such things rather than just reacting to them, the more ease and good feelings you can bring into your life.

> *A loving heart is the truest wisdom.*
>
> CHARLES DICKENS

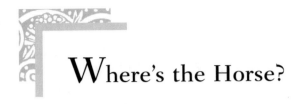

Where's the Horse?

Once upon a time, two little boys were walking through a field. Suddenly one of them stumbled and fell into a pile of horse manure, and the other, who was right behind his friend, fell into it too. The first little boy got up, disgusted, brushing his clothes off, moaning and grousing and generally proclaiming his unhappiness, while the second boy started running wildly around the field. "What is wrong with you?" the first boy asked, "you crazy or something? What are you running around for?" "The horse!" proclaimed the second boy. "I'm looking for the horse!" "What do you mean?" asked the first boy. "Well, if there's a pile of manure here, there's gotta be a horse nearby!" the second boy replied, happily grinning and running looking for the horse.

And so it is in life. Some of us, upon stepping into a pile of manure, see only the manure. Others look for the horse. "Cute story, Dr. Noelle," you say, "but what does that have to do with me? I mean if my car breaks down, or I have a fight with my significant other, or my kid is truant from school—where's the horse? All I can see is a bunch of problems I have to take care of." Indeed, these are problems to take care of. However, they are also opportunities to create a more joyous and successful situation for yourself, if you so desire—in other words, if you're willing to go look for the horse.

You see, buried within any problem is an opportunity. When your car breaks down, for example, there's an opportunity for you to look at how you are dealing with the maintenance of your car: Do you maintain things regularly or do you wait for them to break down before attending to such matters? There's an opportunity for you to look at how you deal with unexpected problems generally speaking: Do you panic, diving into a tailspin of "what ifs" that go from mechanical failure of your car to the disintegration of your entire life? There's an opportunity for you to look at how you do or do not ask for help from others: Do you steadfastly refuse to ask for help from others, or do you lean on others constantly for the least little thing?

Being willing to explore any of these (and related) questions will automatically increase your future happiness and success. If, for example, you find you aren't very good about attending to the maintenance of your car, then doing so in the future will decrease breakdowns and the accompanying stress level. If you realize you tend to panic, discovering that gives you the opportunity to learn new ways of dealing with unexpected problems, which in turn will increase your happiness in the future.

When your kid is truant from school, for example, yes, that's a problem and you need to attend to it right away. However, it's also an opportunity to explore what's going on with your child, why she is avoiding school beyond the obvious "All my friends were at the mall and I wanted to go there too." Perhaps you've lost touch with what really matters to your child, perhaps she has concerns she's been reluctant to share, perhaps your child doesn't really see the value of knowledge, maybe the school she attends doesn't give your child real answers to her real problems; all of these are matters you can investigate that may well prevent some very large problems with your child down the road.

"Dr. Noelle," you say, "this all sounds very nice but I haven't got the time to take everything that happens to me and investigate it like that!" Of course you don't—and you don't need to. Rather than thinking of this as a suggestion to examine everything in minute detail, think of it as an attitude to adopt, a different *approach* to the problems that come up. Just asking yourself the questions "Where's the opportunity here? What good might come of this? What might this situation alert me to that I otherwise wouldn't have noticed?" is enough to get your mind going in a different and more profitable direction.

You'll find that you panic less, that problems seem less horrifying, and that you feel more empowered in your world as you take this approach. Take advantage of the problems life hands you on a platter to point you to happier, more successful ways of living, where there are fewer and fewer "piles of manure" and more and more *bliss*.

A stumble may prevent a fall.

ENGLISH PROVERB

What's the Point?

You are running around madly before work, grabbing a piece of toast, shoving your kids' books, homework, and after-school clothes into backpacks, praying that you have enough gas in the car so you can get the kids to school on time without having to stop for gas first, and suddenly in the midst of it all, a thought flies through your mind, "Why am I doing all this? What's the difference if the kids are late, if I forget their soccer clothes, their homework or some book, what's the point?" Because that's what I'm supposed to do, you think back to yourself, slamming that question down into the depths from whence it came, like who has time to worry about such silly things . . .

Or, you're killing yourself trying to meet the boss's deadline, putting in extra hours, drinking too much coffee and getting too little sleep, and suddenly there's that question again, "Why am I doing this, who cares, what's the point?" and the quick and easy answer flies in, "Because I have to keep my job, duh" and so for now you look no further. Yet as you go about your day, day in, day out, there's that nagging question again "What's the point?" So maybe after the 10:00 news, you finally let yourself really hear the question and realize your usual "because I'm supposed to," or "to keep my job" just isn't cutting it, and, boy, is that depressing.

Good! Most of us go through life "doing"—doing whatever it is that needs to be done: the kids, work, running errands, etc., without looking at why we're doing it beyond the basic necessity of "that's what you gotta do." Yet if what you want out of life isn't just to get through it, but to *enjoy* it, looking beyond the obvious is essential. So congratulations! Your desire for a better answer than "That's the way it is" is the first step to getting there.

Enjoyment happens basically on two levels: sensation and meaning. Either you enjoy something because it feels good to your senses (tastes good, smells good, looks good, etc.) or you enjoy something because it has meaning for you. "Four wheels and a way to get about town" may be a necessity, but not necessarily a source of enjoyment. If, however, your (to you) new car (preowned or otherwise) means that you have more money in the bank or means that you've achieved a higher status in life or that you've finally realized a long-held dream, having that car will bring you enjoyment. So, too, getting the kids to school on time well prepared for their day can be either a task (not very enjoyable) or a source of pleasure. It all depends on the meaning you give to whatever it is you "do."

Meaning, you see, is not automatic. Meaning is the wonderfully individual significance a person gives to something. What you do for your kids, for example, can either be a right royal pain in the neck, a constant source of aggravation, or can be your willing and happy contribution to the success of their future lives. It all depends on how you define the significance of what you do. If you define doing whatever it takes to meet the boss's deadline as simply part of what you have to do, part of your job, your enjoyment will be minimal. If, however, you define your extra time and work as contributing to the overall productivity of the company or contributing to the happiness of the client, or to your next promotion, then you can feel good about what you are doing and thus increase your enjoyment. So much of what we enjoy and don't hinges around the significance we give to it. Even exercising can be "I have to stay thin," hating it all the way, or it can be "I'm giving my body what it needs so I can feel good and be healthy," a source of pride and pleasure.

"What's the point?" is an important question. When you find it coming up, it's probably because you've either forgotten to give significance to something, or it is time to change the significance, find a new and more appealing one. Be good to yourself. Don't just "go through the motions." Give the significance to things that will allow you to live life with the pleasure and joy you deserve.

> *Affirmation of life is the spiritual act by which man ceases to live unreflectively and begins to devote himself to his life with reverence in order to raise it to its true value. To affirm life is to deepen, to make more inward, and to exalt the will to live.*
>
> ALBERT SCHWEITZER

Whose Life Is It Anyway?

There you are, sitting in a rowdy bar on a Friday afternoon after work, not because you particularly want to, but because "Hey, it's happy hour, everybody goes." Or you've been in the same job for 15 years, not because you particularly like it, but because that's the job you got on leaving school, that's what you're trained for, and—that's that. Or you've always seen to it that you are in a relationship, even when you're not all that interested in being in one, or even in the other person, because "everybody has a relationship," and surely you'd be beyond weird if you didn't. But you have this vague sense of constant discomfort, nothing you can really put your finger on, just this funny feeling that makes you want to ask, "Is this all there is to it? Is this all that life is about?"

Well, it depends. It depends on whose life you are living. If you are living a life you have consciously chosen, then life is about a great deal more. The problem is when you live life by default, that is to say, live life according to someone else's choices, not your own.

"Huh?" you say. "That's nonsense, no one tells me what to do!" Really? Then what are you doing spending happy hour being anything but happy? Why in the world are you performing a job you don't particularly like? And whose choices are you living when you get into relationships because "everyone has one"?

One of the great joys of growing up is being able to do what you want to do when you want to do it. The sad thing is, few of us remem-

116

ber that when we become adults. We continue to behave as if we had to let someone else make our choices for us, be that an internalized parent voice saying "you have to," or our willingness to listen to others tell us how to live our lives.

Rebel! Establish your own guidelines for how you want to live your life. It is really OK, and it is a great deal more satisfying. For example, let's say you don't like happy hour, or bridal showers, or concerts, or whatever else it is you feel you "have to" go along with. Challenge yourself to come up with solutions that work for you. How else can you get a sense of belonging, how else can you create a network of friendships? Perhaps you can start a lunch club with fellow employees or make special time to celebrate your friend's upcoming wedding in a more individual way, for example. Be willing to be different; in other words, be willing to live the life that fits you, not the one others think you should live.

If you don't like your job, either redesign how you do your job so you do find satisfaction in it or retrain for a job you will enjoy. Just because *Cosmo* says you should always be in a relationship or *Esquire* implies the man without a weekend date is not a man doesn't make it so. When you go to your grave, the only person who will really care about how you lived your life is—you! Figure out what matters to you, what brings you happiness in the long as well as the short term, and have the courage to create a personalized life.

In the process, ask yourself not just "What do I want" or "What makes me happy," but also "Does this fit with who I am *becoming?*" You see, once you're an adult, you are in charge of your growing up. And it is good to remain conscious of that fact and keep yourself growing the way you want to. Otherwise, you will simply grow willy-nilly in any old direction, much like a garden weed. If you ask "Does this fit with whom I am *becoming?*" you make choices for yourself in the direction you want to be growing in, thus assuring not just current happiness, but future happiness as well.

The answer to "Whose life is it anyway?" is most gratifying when it is a resounding "Mine!" Be willing to live according to who you are— the rewards will astound you.

> *Each player must accept the cards life deals him or her. But once they are in hand, he or she alone must decide how to play the cards in order to win the game.*
>
> VOLTAIRE

Mining for Gold

"Downsizing" sounds like just one of those fancy made-up kind of words, until it happens to you. Then you realize the awful certainty of what it means—fired. "Getting older" just sounds like something that happens naturally to all of us, until you realize it also means companies don't want to hire you; they'd rather go with that fresh-faced 27-year-old (which you were not so very long ago), and suddenly life gets very scary. Your security seems precarious, and the lifestyle you've worked so hard to acquire looks as if it's going down the drain.

If life in the twenty-first century is full of marvels and "better living through technology," for many of us, it's also full of constant change and chaos. The likelihood of losing your job, or your company—even your particular type of work—going out of existence are great. The skills you learned are likely to become outdated way before you're ready for it, and the number of people vying for your job is likely to go up, not down. In the face of such realities, life can feel mightily insecure, and the amount of Maalox consumed goes up exponentially. Short of tightening the belt unbearably or moving to the wilds hoping to "live off the land," what do you do? How do you continue to live a happy and successful life?

1. *Mine for the gold.* That is, the inner gold, the qualities that lie beneath the skills you have learned or the trade you practice. Those qualities are, for example, the self-discipline you've acquired, the creativity you've brought to the surface, the focus and concentration

you've developed over the years. Those qualities are the ability to listen, the patience, the perseverance, the persistence that have evolved as you have met the various challenges of your life. These qualities, and many more, are the gold that underlies your more obvious skills and the "what I know how to do." These are the qualities you need to become aware of and thus be able to call on and use when faced with the need to go in new directions.

2. *Discover your talents.* Look for your deeper talents, the general talents that support your specific abilities. For example, you have a talent, a gift for communicating with others. This meant in your former job, you were a good manager. You can apply that talent for communication to many areas, not just to managing. If management options are limited, figure out other ways, other jobs, in which you can use your talent as a communicator. Think of your talent as your strength, your main support, just as the trunk of a tree is its main support, and the various jobs that could come out of that talent as the branches of a tree, many and varied.

3. *Be flexible.* One of the most critical findings of the research that has been done on those who survived "downsizing" and went on to greater success is their willingness to be flexible. People who said things like "I'm a middle manager, I've always been a middle manager, so I have to find new work as a middle manager" were least likely to be successful. Those who were willing to say, "I've always been a middle manager, I'd like to find new work as a middle manager, but I'm open to doing something quite different" were most likely to succeed. Expanding your options is bound to lead to greater opportunities for success. Remaining flexible is much easier when you are basing that flexibility on your underlying qualities and talents. You are not starting from scratch (which can be really terrifying) but rather are looking for yet another way to express those unique qualities and talents that are profoundly yours.

Chaos and change are not about to leave our lives. The ability to respond to an ever evolving workplace in ways that increase your chances of success and happiness are what winning is all about.

> *There is but one cause of human failure and that is man's lack of faith in his true Self.*
>
> WILLIAM JAMES

The Blame Game

Blaming can be such a satisfying game, at least for a while: "It's not my fault I can't get a job—the economy's rotten." "It's not my fault I can't have a relationship—all the 'good ones' are taken." "It's not my fault my presentation failed—I had a lousy budget for slides and graphics." Certainly at the moment it feels good to put the burden of our failure on somebody else's shoulder, but it doesn't last. Griping never really makes anybody feel good, in the sense of making you feel joyous and happy. It just temporarily numbs out the pain of failure.

Then there's the other approach to blame, the "It's all my fault" approach: "I'm a terrible person, that's why I don't have a good relationship." "I'm stupid and inept, that's why I lost my job." "I'm clumsy and tongue-tied, that's why my presentation failed." This isn't much more satisfying than the "It's-somebody-else's-fault" approach. Whining isn't any better a road to joy than griping.

Most important, neither blaming others nor blaming self actually solves the problem. Yet so many of us, faced with disappointment or failure, resort to blaming, rather than getting off the blame game into the real heart of the matter, solving the problem.

"How convenient for you," you say, "to take a high moral position. You're not the one who was stuck in a terrible relationship/job/situation that absolutely was NOT your fault!" you declare. OK, but where does it get you to focus all your energies on blaming? Yourself or the other? You see, blaming stops the solution process. Instead, focus on *accountability* and *responsibility.*

Accountability is your willingness to assess the part of the problem that belongs to you and the part that belongs to the other. Responsibility is your willingness and ability to respond to that for which you are accountable.

"Which means?" you ask. Which means that you always have a share in the situations you live. This may sound like bad news, but actually it's very good news. The more you are accountable for what's going on in your life, the more powerful you are. The more powerful you are, the more you can transform your life into the life you really want.

However, "be accountable" does not mean "blame yourself." "Be accountable" means figure out realistically what are the *specific* ways in which you've allowed or contributed to the situation. "I'm a terrible person" is a nonspecific statement that is unrealistic and doesn't even start to say in any meaningful way how you've allowed or contributed to the matter.

In figuring out your accountability, you may indeed find that the economy is rotten (that's what the economy contributes to the accountability mix), but realistically, what have you done, for example, to make yourself as hirable as possible (upgrading skills, approaching jobs creatively, being willing to work a wider range of jobs)? That is your portion of accountability. Terrific! This is something for which you can take responsibility. Good relationships may be less common than you'd like (this is what the nature of relationships contributes to the overall accountability for the situation); what have you done to develop those qualities in yourself, for example, to which a high-relationship-quality individual would be attracted? This is your accountability, which then tells you for what you can be responsible. Your presentation was awful? Then evaluate what you have or have not done to develop your presentation skills (Toastmasters, a speaking class, practicing in front of the mirror), in other words, your accountability, and follow up by taking responsibility.

The more you are willing to quit blaming yourself and/or others for the disappointments and failures in your life, the faster you are on the road to genuine success. Be accountable, be responsible, and watch your happiness soar.

> *A man can fail many times, but he isn't a failure until he begins to blame somebody else.*
>
> JOHN BURROUGHS

Breaking the Self-Pity Habit

Y ou're five years old. Your mother sends you to your room because you pulled the cat's tail. "It's not fair!" you cry out. "Johnny pulled the cat's tail, too, and he didn't have to go to his room!" Your mother pays no attention to your protestations, and off you go, teary and miserable. You curl up in a ball on your bed and feel horribly, sadly sorry for yourself. . . .

You're 15 years old. The principal gives you detention for smoking in the bathroom. "It's not fair!" you cry out. "Jane was smoking, too, you just didn't see it and she didn't get detention!" The principal pays no attention to your protestations, and off you go, teary and miserable. You curl up, huddled over your desk, and feel horribly, sadly sorry for yourself. . . .

You're 35 years old. You've just found out you've been passed over for that promotion you've been longing for and that the young upstart who just joined the company got it instead. "It's not fair!" you mutter to yourself as you crawl back miserably into your cubicle. "I work just as hard as he does, only nobody seems to notice it." You curl up, huddled over your work area, and feel horribly, sadly sorry for yourself. . . .

Self-pity. Self-pity is a balm that soothes the troubled heart when we've been hurt and feel we can do nothing about it. Self-pity is the emotional equivalent of taking a drink: Alcohol numbs pain, takes the edge off things. So too does self-pity. And when you're five, self-pity is often the only recourse you have. Let's face it, you can't duke it out physically or intellectually at that age. What the big people say goes. Even at 15, you may have little recourse. Oh, you may be able to duke it out, but the bottom line still is, whatever the grown-ups say is what will happen to you. But by the time you hit 25, 35, and on, you have lots of recourse. The only problem is, by that age, self-pity may have become such a habit that you use it as your main recourse, forgetting all the other more effective ones you have available to you.

A habit is something we do repetitively. Habits are neither good nor bad, in and of themselves. But habits, like anything else, at some point get outdated, lose their effectiveness, cease to be useful to us.

Habits need to be reexamined every so often, to make sure they are indeed serving us in the best way possible.

Self-pity is the licking of wounds. "Poor me, poor me, poor me" does make us feel temporarily better. But that's all it does. Self-pity doesn't do anything toward healing the hurt, fixing the problem, or bettering our lives. If anything, self-pity continued over any period of time makes the problem worse, the hurt worse, and makes your life go downhill. You see, self-pity wraps a protective layer around you, "Poor me, poor me, poor me." You allow only those thoughts and feelings that are in agreement with your self-evaluation of "Poor me" to seep through that protective layering. So from "Poor me" we often go to "It's all their fault." Anytime you place responsibility for a situation entirely outside yourself, you also place the ability to remedy the situation entirely outside yourself. That's a very disempowering thing to do. And past childhood, an unnecessary one.

You are a strong and worthy person. Take back your power. Notice when you go into "poor me," and don't let "poor me" be the whole of how you take care of yourself when you've felt wronged. Lick your wounds for a few minutes, and then take charge. Figure out what you contributed to the unhappy situation in which you find yourself, or how you allowed it to come to pass, and then do what it takes either to transform the present situation or make sure things turn out differently in the future.

Self-pity is a seductive drug. Don't let it dissipate your considerable power in whiny misery.

You are today where your thoughts have brought you; you will be tomorrow where your thoughts take you.

JAMES ALLEN

The Value of Intuition

An expert in the area of personal security, terrorism, stalking, and other such matters, Gavin de Becker has often remarked that people generally sense a potentially dangerous situation or person before the danger actually happens. For example, a woman is waiting for an elevator; when the doors open, there's a man already inside the elevator, and the woman has an instinctive fearful reaction to that individual. However, Mr. de Becker goes on to say, 99 times out of a 100, the woman will say to herself "Oh, that's silly, it's just my imagination" or "I'm certainly not going to let him think I'm scared by not getting on the elevator" and proceeds to close herself up in a metal box alone with a stranger she's afraid of. Unfortunately, too often, her fear was justified and the woman is assaulted.

All of us have intuition, that quiet inner voice that gives us a sense of a situation or a person long before our minds have had the time to process what's going on. Intuition comes under many headings: "instinctive reaction," "gut feeling," "premonition," "vibes." What all of them have in common is that you can't logically describe what makes the feeling or how your intuition comes about; all you know is you feel it.

A human being is a wholistic mechanism. We operate as a whole system (body, mind, heart, soul) where the different parts interact so as to perform most effectively as one. The overvaluing of the rational mind so prevalent in our century and the Western world leaves out matters of heart and soul. If something isn't logical, if we can't explain it and understand precisely how it works, we don't want to hear about it. In the process, we cut ourselves off from information that although not rational or explainable is critical to our survival and our greater fulfillment. Intuition is most definitely of the heart and soul. There is nothing rational about intuition—except not using it. It isn't logical to fail to take advantage of such potentially valuable information. Yet we fail to do so regularly. Why?

1. *We don't listen.* Becoming sensitive to your intuition or gut feelings about things requires a willingness to listen to and for that intuition. Often it means just being quiet for a moment and "listening" to your inner self. Or, should you just get a "gut feeling" about someone or something out of the blue, taking a moment to recognize the feeling. Your gut feelings won't always be fearful ones. Sometimes you'll get a "don't-go-there" or "something-fishy-here" sense, both of which are avoidance or caution signals, but sometimes you'll get a sense that "this is a great idea" or "oh, I feel excited about this," both of which are "explore further" signals from your inner self. Some people believe their intuition is a spiritual voice guiding them. Whichever is most appropriate for you—inner voice or divine voice—listen to it.

2. *We don't act on the feeling.* Too often, once we've had an intuition, a gut feeling, we ignore it. We say, like the woman waiting for the elevator, "Oh, it's just my imagination" rather than recognizing and honoring that intuition as just as valid an information-gathering device as the rational mind. Or we deny its value: "Well, I certainly won't let him know I'm scared" and proceed to act without taking into account the intuitive information so as to protect ourselves.

Intuition, like anything else, needs to be exercised to become strong. Think of it as an inner muscle. If you don't use it, it becomes weak and atrophied, thus hard to hear. Instead, respect your intuition, act on it, and don't care what others may think of your decision to do so. For example, if your intuition says "Don't take the freeway today," take an alternate route. Some days you will be surprised to find out there was a major accident on the freeway, and you would have been in traffic for hours had you taken your usual route. Other days, nothing may have apparently happened. It doesn't matter. If, indeed, sometimes all you are respecting is your overdeveloped imagination, so what! In the process you will be strengthening your intuition so that over time, you will be increasingly hearing valuable messages, information that may very well be lifesaving.

> *Trust your hunches. They're usually based on facts filed away just below the conscious level.*
>
> DR. JOYCE BROTHERS

Stuff Happens

Stuff happens. Somebody keys your car when it's just sitting there in the supermarket parking lot; you set your briefcase down for a second to blow your nose, and your briefcase is gone—stolen; vandals have picked your house as target practice and broken all your windows; you yell out to the heavens, "What is going on? Why is this happening to me? What did I do to deserve this?" You're angry, frustrated, and hurt. You become paranoid, fearful, and distrusting. You begin thinking you must be doing something to attract such bad experiences. You feel stupid, inept, a "loser."

And serious stuff happens. Your spouse is diagnosed with a terminal illness, your brother is murdered in a drive-by, your child is paralyzed by a drunk driver's hit and run . . . and your cry is more intense, "Why is this happening to me? What did I do to deserve this? How could God let this happen?" You are agonized, outraged, and in despair. You turn inward, finding life ugly and unpleasant. You curse at a God who allows such awfulness. You don't want to live.

Stuff happens, serious stuff. Your cries are natural, understandable. The problem lies not in our original reactions—our anger, our pain, our cries to what feels like a cold and uncaring God/Goddess. These are all normal reactions to such experiences. The true damage is done when we allow that reaction to determine our *response*.

You see, you can't do much about the "stuff" that has happened. What is done, is done. There's no way to "undo" it. Wrapping your response tightly around the past event serves only to prolong your own pain, to reinforce your anger. By becoming paranoid, fearful, and distrusting, for example, you hurt yourself. Your desire to protect yourself is a worthy one, but because you are doing so reactively ("I won't trust anybody, they are all out to get me"), you constrict your freedom, you shut out the possibility of good as well as bad experiences. "Great," you reply, "so what am I supposed to do? Leave myself wide open for everyone in town to steal from me?" No. Recognize the need to protect yourself from future hurt, but by being *proactively creative,* not by being paranoid. Find out from the local police station, for example, if there have been other instances of cars vandalized ("keyed") or any other minor criminal activity in the area of your supermarket, and if so, shop at a different supermarket, and/or park closer to lit entrances, and get your neighbors to sign a complaint petition to submit to your local police and elected officials demanding better crime control.

Don't fault yourself for past occurrences; instead, sort out where you can take responsibility and take better care of yourself in the future. For example, thinking you've done something "bad" to attract such bad experiences does nothing to protect you in the future, and only sinks your self-esteem. Labeling yourself "stupid, inept, a loser" has no usefulness. All it does is undermine your ability to actually do something constructive for yourself. Instead, figure out, for example, "OK, setting my briefcase down for any reason in a busy public place isn't a good idea. If I need to blow my nose (or whatever), I'll just start setting it down between my feet (rather than by my side), where it's harder to get at." Terrific! Now you've protected yourself without damning the rest of the human race. That is a helpful response.

So too with the "serious" stuff. Many wonderful causes have been undertaken by people who have suffered hideous tragedy. "M.A.D.D." (Mothers Against Drunk Drivers), now a powerful national organization that has successfully lobbied for laws against drunk drivers, was begun by one woman who lost her child to a drunk driver.

Christopher Reeve, who could just have nursed his pain in private, is using his tragic paralysis to bring public attention and funds to much needed research for spinal-cord injuries. The list goes on and on. These are valiant and beautiful proactive responses to past tragedy. After you've cried your tears and screamed out your anger, heal your pain by doing whatever you can so that others don't need to suffer as you have. Oddly, contributing to others' well-being is one of the most powerful ways to contribute to your own.

> *Do not let what you cannot do interfere with what you can do.*
>
> JOHN WOODEN

Talk Less, Listen More

You moan, you groan, you are beyond frustration with your significant other, whom you can't seem to get to do ANYTHING you need him to do; and then there's your child (who you have decided couldn't possibly be your child, they must have made a mistake at the hospital—of course, your child is sitting there thinking the same thing . . .) who absolutely refuses to do what she is supposed to do, AND, you continue, still at top volume, there's your co-worker/employee who stubbornly will not go along with his part of your current project. "Life has its frustrations," I respond. "Oh, that's real helpful," you say. "What am I supposed to do!" you yell, quickly adding me to your list of frustrations.

Good question. Maybe you're not supposed to "do" much of anything. Maybe the whole problem has been your seeing only one way to resolve your frustrations, namely demanding, pushing, or nudging (all of which are one form or another of "doing") people to do what you need done.

"So what's the answer?" you ask, thoroughly irritated. "Am I just supposed to give up? Let them do nothing? Do it all myself?" Giving up won't get the job done, letting "them" do nothing will only make you resentful, and doing it all yourself will earn you an early grave as you drive yourself prematurely into it. So, no. Instead, talk less, listen more, and prepare more.

1. *Listen more.* When people resist doing either what they've agreed to do, or what they are "supposed" to do, it's rarely because they

truly don't want to do it under any circumstances. Most of the time, it's because there is something about doing the thing you need done that doesn't work for them.

"Great," you say, "so why don't they say so?" For about a hundred different reasons, none of which matter right now. What does matter is that you have a way to find out what their resistance is. Ask, for example, "It seems to be difficult for you to do your share of the housework. What's in the way for you?" The phrase "What's in the way?" is a very nonjudgmental, effective question. Ask genuinely, really wanting to know the answer, without anger, without attacking, and then listen. Don't accept "I don't know" as an answer; ask again, gently, nicely, "Well, if you did know, what might be in the way of your getting this done?" And listen. Accept the answer you get, "I don't have the time." Don't debate it. One of the reasons people are reluctant to share their reticence to doing things is our tendency to argue with them ("What do you mean you don't have time! You have time to watch the football game!"). Once you've determined what the resistance is, find out what his preference is: "OK, well, how can we work it out so either you do find the time or we figure out another way to get the housework done?" And once again—listen.

When we stop blaming people, faulting them, and generally making them wrong for having their preferences and resistances, people become much more willing to share their reasoning with us and become open to working out solutions with us. Who wants to be cooperative with a screaming, demanding person or a whining, pleading, nagging, begging one? Neither are conducive to working out solutions together.

Children are people too. You'll get a lot more cooperation from your children when you approach them as people with their own preferences and resistances. If you are open to hearing and accepting those, then your child will be more open to working with you to get things done.

2. *Prepare more.* Once you've listened, you may want to think for a while in order to take into account the other person's preferences and resistances with what you need to get done. Don't be overly eager to jump to a new solution. Think it through, be willing to come back with two or three new solutions, factoring in the other person's preferences. Ask him to come up with two or three of his own; then when you meet again to work it through, you can use elements from both your "lists of solutions." People are much more willing to go along with decisions in which they have had an active hand. (And yes, once again, children are people too.)

If you only look at what is, you might never attain what could be.

UNKNOWN

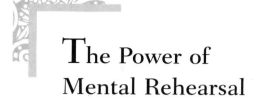

The Power of
Mental Rehearsal

Over the past few years, psychologists have become increasingly aware of the powerful influence the mind has over emotions and the body. For example, psychologists have had remarkable success using mental imagery to contain such life-threatening conditions as cancer. In sports psychology, visualizations are an integral part of training for Olympic athletes. Before a race, for example, an Olympic runner will mentally rehearse her race over and over and over again in her imagination. In doing so, the runner is using the power of her subconscious and unconscious minds to help her win.

"Very nice, Dr. Noelle," you say, "but what does this have to do with me?" Well, you know that presentation you have to make? To sell the product, get the client, close the deal? Or that conversation you're dreading with your boss to get that raise? Or with your friend to work out that problem between you? That's where mental rehearsal can be of use to you. You see, running a race or hurling a javelin is no different in essence to the challenge you face. Much is riding on this moment, and you need to do your best to win. Mental rehearsal can help.

Here's how you do it:

1. *Sit or lie down in a quiet spot.* Find one where you will not be interrupted, but be careful not to go to sleep. You need to be relaxed and comfortable, not unconscious. Loosen any clothes that are tight, take off your glasses, your watch, make yourself pleasantly comfortable.

Close your eyes, take a few deep breaths, and then relax all your muscles. Start at your feet and work your way up to your head, one muscle group at a time. Then take a nice deep breath and relax your muscles from the top of your head back down to the bottom of your feet. You should feel very relaxed.

2. *Take a deep breath.* Now start to visualize in your mind the situation in which you will be. For example, see yourself walking into your boss's office, make a mental image of yourself calm and happy, feeling good about yourself and the raise for which you're about to ask. Feel strong and self-confident, excited about asking for your raise. Feel prepared, feel the good feelings of your preparation paying off as you are able to give the boss positive reasons for your raise and how they will benefit the company. See yourself talking to your boss in a firm and positive manner.

3. See your boss *responding* to you with equal positiveness and enthusiasm. During the entire visualization be sure to really *feel* the desired emotions as vividly as you can. Engaging your emotions is the key to a successful mental rehearsal. Visualize your boss on your side, giving you the raise you want. See yourself leaving the boss's office happy and satisfied. See yourself later on the telephone with your best friend or significant other, and hear them congratulating you on your success. Feel the happiness and joy of success flood your whole being.

The more important the situation you are facing, the more ahead of time you should begin your "rehearsal" and the more times you should do it. So begin "rehearsing" a week ahead of time, for example, and "rehearse" once a day before an important presentation. Just doing a single session of mental rehearsal the night before an important discussion, however, is extremely valuable. Doing visualizations before sleep seems to work particularly well.

If you're in a bind and you have literally just a few minutes before an important event, then take a few moments in the privacy of the restroom to close your eyes and quickly rehearse the situation the way you want it to come out for you.

Mental rehearsal can make the difference between feeling deep down like you know what you're doing versus being insecure and worried about the chances of your success. Mental rehearsal reinforces your qualities and strong points, boosts your self-confidence and self-esteem, and helps you think creatively in a positive mode. It helps keep all parts of you—conscious, subconscious, and unconscious—on the same track by focusing your thoughts and emotions on one thing: success. Remember, though: The magic of mental rehearsal is not to be substituted for thorough preparation and "knowing your stuff." Mental rehearsal cannot invent what is not there. If you have not prepared an excellent "show," there is nothing to rehearse. This being said, when you put excellent preparation together with mental rehearsal—success is easily and readily yours.

Success has a simple formula: Do your best, and people may like it.

SAM EWING

Approval vs. Love

When you start developing a new love relationship, there's always the hope that this is the one, that this particular relationship will last, that this time you'll find love, happiness, and fulfillment. And all too often, you're disappointed. Something happens, something goes wrong, and either the person doesn't turn out to be who you thought he was or you don't feel loved the way you thought you would. Among all the other reasons things go wrong in a relationship, one of the most prevalent and least recognized is our tendency to confuse approval with love.

Approval is when someone is pleased with something you've said or done. You like your hamburgers medium well, the waiter brings you a hamburger medium well, you approve of it. You tell your dog "Sit and stay," he does, you pat him on the head—you approve. Approval is a feedback mechanism that lets us and others know how we're doing.

In the beginning of a relationship, you need feedback to let you know if you and this new person are going to get along. The problem is that instead of using whatever feedback you get as information regarding the potential for happiness in this relationship, you want love so badly that you force the feedback to be favorable by seeking approval. You deliberately do things you figure the person will like, and sure enough you get approval. Feels great; you think things are going fine. Then you do something he doesn't approve of, and rather than stopping and thinking: "What does this disapproval tell me about the future of this relationship?" you panic and think, "He's not going to love me anymore," and you quickly drop/hide the disapproved behavior. All too often, you end up dropping/hiding more and more behaviors until you are no longer yourself, and you become angry, bitter, and resentful, leading to the inevitable downfall of the relationship.

Approval isn't love. Just because a person approves of who and what you are or do doesn't mean he loves you. Love is much more complex than that. Love is caring about the other person as he is, valuing him as he is, seeking to know and understand him as he is, and finding ways to be yourself harmoniously with his as your true selves.

You can't find out who a person is, nor can you allow him to know and understand you, if you keep falsifying the feedback. Be true to yourself. Be who you are and trust that there is someone out there who wants to love you as you are. Look for that person by noticing how people respond to you when you're being genuinely you. Use people's approval and disapproval not as the guidelines for how you should behave, but as feedback as to whether or not a relationship with a person who approves of X part of you and disapproves of Y would be a healthy and happy relationship.

Let approval be a useful servant to you in its feedback role, and help you find the LOVE you deserve.

We don't love qualities, we love a person; sometimes by reason of their defects as well as their qualities.

JACQUES MARITAIN

The Choice for Love

Fear is the great spoiler of joy. Fear stands in the way of enjoyment, peace, and serenity. Fear runs enormous portions of our lives—often without our realizing it—and causes great internal damage. And yup, too often fear is there, a constant pal and buddy, from the moment that alarm clock rings in the morning.

You've set the alarm because you're afraid you'll get up late otherwise. You shower and apply deodorant because you're afraid you'll offend others if you don't. You drive at the speed limit because you're afraid the cop three cars behind will give you a ticket if you go any faster, and you arrive at work on time because you're afraid if you're late, you'll be fired. You do your work meeting your deadlines and quota because you're afraid you'll lose your job if you don't. You eat "rabbit food" for lunch because you're afraid you'll get fat if you eat anything else. You rush home to take care of the kids/spouse/pets because you're afraid if you don't they'll be getting in trouble/angry/neglected. You catch the evening news as you get ready for bed because you're afraid you'll miss something important otherwise. You try to make sure you get eight hours' sleep because you're afraid you'll feel awful if you don't. And you wonder why you feel tense all the time, when really everything in your life is going just fine.

Don't despair—there is an alternative. Love. Not a mushy, airy-fairy concept of "love," but a real, practical, down-to-earth valuing of self and others that can literally transform your life.

For example, set the alarm because you care about your well-being so much you want to face the day in timely fashion. Shower and apply deodorant because being clean and smelling nice feels good to you. Drive at the speed limit because you know that the speed limit was created to keep us all safe, yourself included, and you value your life and that of others. Arrive at work on time because you enjoy honoring your agreements. Do your work meeting your deadlines and quota because you enjoy feeling the satisfaction of a job well done. Eat your carefully selected "rabbit food" for lunch because you value your health and enjoy looking a certain way. Get home without rushing in time to take care of the kids/spouse/pets because you enjoy taking care of and interacting with your loved ones. Watch the evening news as you get ready for bed because you like to keep current on what's going on in the world. Make sure you get eight hour's sleep because you care about yourself and wish to ensure a happy, refreshed wake-up.

The content of your day doesn't change; you still get up at 7:00, shower, go to work, and so forth; what changes is how you view that content. You do that by systematically asking yourself throughout the day, "Am I doing this because I'm afraid of what might happen if I don't? Or am I doing this out of love for myself and others or to create pleasure, enjoyment, and good feelings?"

Make the choice for love and watch your life transform as if by magic before your eyes.

---

*T*hings do not change, we do.

HENRY DAVID THOREAU

Enabling vs. Helping

There has been much talk about "codependency" in the past few years. It is now widely recognized that friends and families of people with various addictive/dysfunctional behaviors are frequently "codependent," meaning that by what they do and say, friends and family enable people to continue their addictive/dysfunctional behavior. For example, when you make excuses or cover up for an addicted/rageful/battering spouse's inappropriate behavior, you are enabling, or making it easy for your spouse to continue being addicted/rageful/battering. Your spouse doesn't have to face the consequences of his/her inappropriate behavior and therefore doesn't have any reason to behave any differently.

Where friends and family get confused is that they go from not wanting to enable someone's addiction or other inappropriate behavior to figuring, "Well, it looks as if helping someone is what makes you an enabler, so I'm not going to help anyone at all."

There is a vast difference between enabling and helping. Enabling is helping a person in a way that feeds his/her dysfunction. Helping is being there for someone in a way that does not support his/her dysfunction. Enabling in the preceding example is making excuses; helping is accompanying your spouse to his/her first AA meeting.

However, figuring out what is helping versus what is enabling often is much more complex than "making excuses versus accompanying to AA meeting" and requires careful evaluation. This is why many people give up and just stop helping in general. For example, sometimes helping involves some enabling. Let's say your spouse can't go to the AA meeting because she is so hungover she can't see straight to drive. Yes, driving her there does allow her to drink and still go to AA meetings. In that respect it is enabling. However, you have faith that if your spouse attends meetings eventually she will receive the support she needs to heal herself. In that respect, driving her to the meeting is helpful.

How to resolve this dilemma? Tell your spouse what you are doing. Give her consequences and hold to them: "I have faith in you and in the support you get at AA to heal yourself; however, I will not continue to help you get there when you're hungover. Being hungover is your responsibility, and you get to deal with it. I will drive you there today. I will not drive you there again under the same circumstances." And stick to your guns. Your spouse will undoubtedly test your resolve. If you refuse, while reaffirming your faith in her and suggesting alternatives—"I have faith in you and your ability to heal yourself, and I'm so glad AA is a good place for you, and I won't drive you there since the reason you want me to is you're too hungover to drive there yourself. I will help you think of ways to get there on your own. I love you"—you are helping, not enabling. You are giving her an opportunity and the loving support to take charge of her own healing.

Helping is wonderful and valuable. Enabling is not. Be truly "there" for friends and loved ones by caring enough to help—without enabling.

---

*R*esponsibility is the price of greatness.

WINSTON CHURCHILL

On Choosing Enthusiasm

Have you ever been to a party where one of the guests comes in with a sour face, and no matter how much fun everybody else is having, he finds fault with whatever is going on, criticizes everything and everybody, and puts a damper on the whole event? Or you're in a perfectly good mood and you start talking with someone who sees nothing but doom and gloom in the world and within minutes you get depressed? We call such people "party-poopers" or "downers." Nobody likes to be around them, with good reason. But have you ever thought about what *you* bring to the party? In other words, what do you bring to your life? Do you consistently bring excitement, enthusiasm, caring, wonder, and appreciation to your life? Or do you whine a lot, complaining, moaning, and finding something wrong with most everything?

What you bring to your life is what you receive in return. For example, if you approach your work with enthusiasm, you'll find it easier to do, more fun, and consequently, you'll be more successful. But, ah, you say, there's nothing to get enthusiastic about in my work. No? How about getting enthusiastic about the people who directly or indirectly benefit from what you do. Or that society functions more smoothly or better because of what you do, or that you can afford to pay your rent because of your job, or that you can use this job as a stepping-stone to a better job. There's always something you can find to be enthusiastic about if you look hard enough. And if there really is nothing to get enthusiastic about, quit! Life's too precious to live it without joy.

What you bring to your life applies to the little things as well as to the big things. For example, it's easy to see how bringing enthusiasm, caring, and appreciation to your relationships will pay off in joy and love. It's not always obvious how the same principle applies to the smaller things, such as traffic or going to the dentist, yet they do.

For example, if you get in your car, complaining about the smog, how awful the drive home will be, it's too hot out, and it's rush hour, oh, how you hate it, you will experience the drive through the filter of those expectations. Does this mean you have to be enthusiastic and excited about getting in the smog, heat, and rush hour? No, of course not, that would be downright masochistic. Transform your experience of the drive by finding something you can be genuinely enthusiastic about, all the while being aware of and acknowledging the smog, heat, and rush hour and choosing not to focus on them.

Knowing you have to spend two hours getting home instead of one, get enthusiastic about listening to your favorite radio station and relaxing as you take the slow drive. Get enthusiastic about finding a new route home and really look at the neighborhoods you go through with appreciation and curiosity, wondering who lives here, what kind of people I think these are, what their lives are like.

You do get what you give. Give the best of you—you'll be amazed at how great life gets.

Life is the movie you see through your own, unique eyes. It makes little difference what's happening out there. It's how you take it that counts.

DENNIS WAITLEY

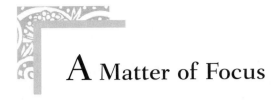

A Matter of Focus

Whatever you focus on grows. Wherever you put your attention and energy will determine what happens in your life. If you focus on being kind and loving, not manipulatively in order to get something, but just because you enjoy being kind and loving, kind and loving things will happen in your life. If you focus on your grievances, and on the feeling that "people are out to get me," indeed, you will experience many grievances.

The nature of focus, however, is often misunderstood. Let's say you want to increase the loving experiences in your life, but an event happens that makes you angry. You want to "focus on the loving in my life," so you deny your anger or push it away. That's certainly a valiant attempt at keeping your focus on loving, but it is misunderstanding the nature of focus and will only cause you problems down the line.

Focus is where you concentrate your energy, what you do with something once you've noticed it. For example, someone cuts you off on the freeway; this annoys you. Denying that it annoyed you will only put the irritation somewhere else in your mental/emotional/physical system to crop up later as some form of distress. Focusing on your annoyance (concentrating your energy there) will magnify it until you are a raging, fuming maniac hating everyone on the road. Instead of either denying or focusing on your annoyance—

1. *Acknowledge the reality of the event.* You got cut off; it is annoying.

2. *Allow yourself to feel your annoyance.* Express it appropriately in the moment (that is, by saying to yourself forcefully, "I'm annoyed!"); then, your emotion being released, get off it, and

3. *Concentrate your energy (focus) on loving values.* Do so if loving experiences are what you want to increase in your life. For example, focus on your thankfulness that most drivers don't cut others off, or use the event as a reminder to pay extra attention to the road because you care about yourself and others' well-being too much to drive carelessly.

Or, to use another example: Your boss yells at you; you feel hurt and angry. Using the preceding guidelines, you would neither deny your emotion, "Oh, my boss, he just gets that way, it's nothing, I just love him to death" (right!), nor allow your feelings to magnify to where you storm in the office, slam your fist on his desk, and announce in rageful tears, "I quit." Instead—

1. *Acknowledge the reality of the event.* He yelled at you; you are hurt and mad.

2. *Allow yourself to feel your feelings and express them appropriately in the moment.* Go into the rest room and pace and fume for however long it takes you to release the emotion.

3. *Concentrate your energy (focus) on loving values.* You appreciate this opportunity to figure out a better way of doing whatever it is that displeased your boss and go about doing that. You are grateful your boss values you so much he yelled at you rather than fired you.

The ability to concentrate our energies is a wonderful and powerful gift. Choose where you put your focus wisely, and it will serve you well.

*T*he more things I am grateful for, the more things I find to be grateful about.

FLORENCE SCOVEL SHINN

New Year's Resolution

You've made your New Year's resolution: "That's it, no more Mr. Nice Guy for me! I'm not letting them walk all over me anymore!" and off you go, trampling hearts and chopping heads off, until everyone around you is cowering, fleeing, or resenting the heck out of you. "Well, that didn't work," you say to yourself, scratching your head. "They aren't walking all over me anymore, but they can't stand me either. Forget this." Or your resolution is the opposite: "OK, fine, everyone says I'm like a bull in the china shop, so I'll be nice, I'll be sweet," and then you're furious because nothing ever gets done and people aren't paying attention to you anymore. "Forget this," you say, "I'd rather be heard," and back you go to your bull-in-the-china-shop ways.

Somewhere in all of this you've forgotten what a wonderfully complex individual you are. You've forgotten that you're not 100 percent of any one thing, but that you are made up of many different parts. There's a "nice guy/gal" part to all of us, an aggressive (the "bull-in-the-china-shop") part to all of us, and all sorts of parts in between. Some of those parts are underdeveloped, some overdeveloped, some we use appropriately, some we don't. So the problem isn't that your New Year's resolution is faulty—you're probably on the right track—you just hadn't quite figured out which part of you to use how or when.

For example, if you feel you've been "walked on" by too many people too often, you probably have an underdeveloped aggressive side that you don't use appropriately. You may think that being "strong" means being confrontational, yelling at people, and insisting on getting your way. In fact, that kind of "strong" is just one facet of being aggressive. Other facets of being aggressive would be standing your ground; using a firm, low voice and repetition to communicate to others your position; and learning to negotiate rather than to sacrifice.

If your New Year's resolution is to "be nice," having been forceful and demanding all of your life, your vision of what being "nice" is is probably more a vision of being a doormat. That isn't nice, that's dead! Of course you're not getting what you want. Rather than reverting to your old ways, learn what genuine "niceness" is all about: listening to others, caring about others as much as you do about yourself (not instead of yourself), respecting *both* yours and others' needs.

If your primary approach to life and others isn't working for you, it's probably because you are relying too heavily on what feels comfortable and easy for you in situations where your comfort zone and the situation at hand don't mesh. For example, ordering people around may work when you're the football coach or the police officer, but it's not going to get you anywhere in your personal relationships. For that, you need the part of you that is willing to listen and care. You may have buried that part of you long ago and now fear that listening and caring are part of being "weak." Listening and caring are just as important as the ability to show leadership. Each has its importance. The art of living is in large part the art of knowing when to use which, that is, when to listen and care versus when to lead firmly and directly versus when to do something entirely different.

Don't let your personal comfort zone rule your life. Take an objective look at yourself and recognize which parts of you are underdeveloped. There is more to you than you realize. Develop those unfamiliar sides of yourself that you recognize would be of benefit in certain situations and practice using them. Pay attention to other people. How do other people manage to be aggressive yet not terrorize everyone in sight? How do other people manage to be "nice" without getting walked on? You are a valuable human being. Become more of the whole person you can be and watch your life expand into greater and happier success.

Don't wish it were easier, wish you were better.

JIM BOHN

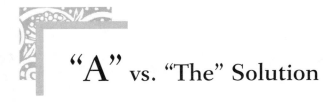

"A" vs. "The" Solution

You've had it. That's the sixth time this month your car has been in the shop, you can't handle it anymore, so what if it's a relatively new car, obviously you bought a lemon (and of course you've owned it beyond the darned "lemon-law" period of time). You decide, "That's it, I don't care what I have to do, I'm getting a new car," and you do! Immediately. You plunk down the initial payment, using next month's rent to do so, and drive happily off for the next few weeks until it dawns on you that you way overcommitted yourself, there's no way you can keep up these payments, and you wish you had your lemon back. . . .

You don't know what to do. You're frozen. You certainly don't want to do anything impulsive (look where that got you), but going on as you have is going to kill your finances. You're between a rock and a hard place.

Well, maybe. It certainly may feel like that, but the truth is you're caught in the trap of looking for "The" solution rather than looking for *a* solution, which in fact may be a series of solutions that eventually get you to your goal.

When a problem feels big, all-engulfing, overwhelming, whether it be dealing with a too-expensive car or the pain of a difficult marriage, our tendency is to look for a big all-encompassing solution. "I'll dump the car," "I'll get out of the marriage," "I'll move." Sometimes those are indeed the best possible solutions, but often you sacrifice all sorts of other things in the process. Dumping your lemon certainly got rid of that problem, but getting the new car brought along a whole host of new problems. Getting out of the marriage quickly gets you out of that pain, but may bring with it divorce issues you hadn't sorted out and must now deal with.

Instead of acting impulsively or freezing into permanent paralysis, think first about the impact "The" solution is likely to have on other parts of your life. What will buying a new car mean, for example? Bigger car payments, let's say. That will have an unhappy impact on your pocketbook. What impact will leaving the marriage have? Finding a new home, coming to monetary agreements, loneliness, child-custody issues, and so on. Now, given your realization of the impact "The" solution will have, rather than running right to it, *deal first with the impact, then come to the solution.*

If you deal first with figuring out where the money will come from for your new car, for example, when you come to actually buying it, you won't be putting yourself in financial jeopardy.

If *before* you leave the painful marriage you figure out where you intend to live, how you will financially do that, what you want in terms of monetary agreements and what you will do if you don't get what you hope for, how you want custody issues to be resolved, and what steps you will need to take to do so, then you will be able to leave the marriage feeling secure about your life ahead, not panicked.

Too often we come at problem solving purely by looking at the problem. If you start by looking first at the impact whatever solution you're considering will have on your life, you will make it much easier for yourself to come up with a solution that "fits" for you. You are also much less likely to find yourself in states of jeopardy, be those financial, physical, or emotional.

Be good to yourself. Don't allow overwhelming problems to overwhelm you. Look for "a" solution (as in a series of), not "The" solution, and watch your problems reduce to surprisingly manageable proportions.

> *Action to be effective must be directed to clearly conceived ends.*
>
> JAWAHARLAL NEHRU

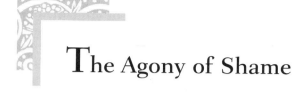

The Agony of Shame

You're interviewing for a new job or a promotion. You're nervous enough as it is, it took you weeks to work up the gumption to come in for the interview, and then the interviewer asks you something mundane like "What do you consider to be your weaknesses?" You're dumb struck, not at the question, it's a very ordinary question to be asked during an interview, but at yourself. You forgot to prepare for this one. You remembered to prepare for "What are your major strengths?" and "Why do you think you should get this job/promotion?" but you forgot all about the weakness category, and there you sit, feeling your face flush hot as you can't think, can't come up with what has to be a good answer, and stammer your way through. The interviewer thanks you politely and sends you on your way. "I blew it!" you say to yourself as you leave, humiliated. "I blew it, and it's all my fault. I should have known that one was coming, I should have prepared for it." And off you slink, riddled with shame.

You're at a family gathering. You're having a good time, enjoying your not-too-often-seen relatives and the conversation. You end up drinking a little more beer than you're used to and get involved in a rather heated discussion about gangs. Somewhere in the middle of it you proclaim rather loudly that kids who join gangs are just a bunch of no-good-niks and so what if the cops don't always respect their rights. A dead silence follows your remark, and you suddenly remember your Aunt Helen lost her son to a police bullet in the confusion of a gang-related incident. You feel that all-too-familiar flush engulf your face and wish you could just disappear. You are mortified at your own insensibility, at forgetting something that important. Off you slink, riddled with shame.

Shame. Healthy shame is a necessary emotion. It's a response to when you've done something you should not have done. Healthy shame is a product of your conscience, and as such is valuable. One of the primary distinguishing characteristics between sociopaths (people who can torture and kill without feeling bad about it) and normal people is that sociopaths do not feel shame and therefore lack remorse.

But what about you? You feel plenty of shame, you inform me. As a matter of fact you feel so much shame, you'd like to just hide your face forever! Indeed. And therein lies the problem. You see, shame is not supposed to be something you drag around behind you forever, like some sort of moralistic ball and chain; shame is supposed to be a warning mechanism, a way your conscience can poke you and say "Hey, you messed up here!" What you *do* with that message is entirely up to you. You're not a child anymore, when your parents dictated what you did in response to that feeling. You're an adult (mercifully) and you get to decide what to do with it. Dragging your shame around behind you so it can slam into your ankles, trip you up, and make you feel like a worthless idiot isn't the most useful approach.

Instead, respond as follows:

1. *Fix the mistake.* This sounds so obvious, yet we often fail to do it. If at all possible, correct whatever it was that led to your feeling ashamed in the first place. Write a letter to the interviewer or ask for a second interview, during which you say something like, "I realized I was not well prepared for your question regarding my weaknesses. I'd like to respond to that now." Worst case, the interviewer will say "No, it's too late." So be it. Use the experience as a reminder to be better prepared for the next interview. With your Aunt Helen, apologize! Take

some sensitivity training or drink less in social settings; in other words, take proactive measures so you don't put yourself in such a shame-producing situation again.

2. *Forgive yourself.* You made a mistake. You're human, it happens. Use shame for the valuable warning device it is, not something with which to whip yourself into self-imposed martyrhood.

> *Running from problems is a sure way of running into problems.*
>
> FROM BITS & PIECES 12/31/98
> (HTTP://WWW.EPINC.COM)

Seven Ways to Say "No" to Sexual Harassment in the Workplace

Sexual harassment thrives on silence and secrecy. As with any kind of abuse, once it is held up to the light of day, the harasser cannot continue his or her inappropriate (and hurtful!) behavior. Your two greatest weapons against sexual harassment are your willingness to speak up loudly and firmly and your willingness to disclose what is going on to those who can take action.

The Fair Employment and Housing Commission defines sexual harassment as "unwanted sexual advances, or visual, verbal or physical conduct of a sexual nature." The person on the receiving end is the one who defines the advance as wanted or unwanted, sexual or nonsexual.

Sexual harassment has no place in our lives. It is demeaning, degrading, and produces anxiety, low self-esteem, and a number of other unwanted emotional, mental, and physical symptoms. If someone is sexually harassing you (and remember, YOU are the one who defines what is sexual harassment for you), take the steps to compel the perpetrator to stop. Don't for one instant think that politely telling a harasser "Gee, that makes me kind of uncomfortable" will do it. Sexual harassment is an assault and needs to be dealt with as such: clearly, firmly, and with determination.

1. *Stand Tall.* Whenever someone by word or gesture does something that makes you feel uncomfortable, draw yourself up as tall as you can, look him or her in the eye, and say in a clear, firm voice

(louder than you would normally speak): "Please don't do that. I don't like it." If he/she laughs or says something like, "I was only joking" or "Come on, lighten up," look him/her in the eye and, standing as tall as you know how, say clearly and directly, "It's not funny to me. I don't want to lighten up. Don't do that. I don't like it."

Don't wait for the harassment to continue; report the incidents immediately.

2. *Educate Yourself.* Know your rights. Every company must have a manual that defines the procedure to follow if you feel you have been sexually harassed. Find out what that procedure is. Educate yourself also about your legal rights in the workplace. Contact the EEOC in Washington, DC (800-669-3362).

3. *Document and Report.* It is in your best interest to report any incident of sexual harassment immediately. If you are not sure if something constitutes sexual harassment, err on the side of caution— *report it.*

Write a brief description of what happened, by and to whom, name of witnesses, where the harassment took place, the date and the time. Whenever you report inappropriate behavior, do so in writing even if written documentation is not required by company policy. Keep a copy of the complaint for yourself.

4. *Honor Your Feelings.* If a behavior or words make you feel uncomfortable, honor your feelings. Don't assume that you are overre-acting and are oversensitive. Take the time to look carefully at what happened and respect your feelings as a valid indicator of what is right for you. Then stand firmly behind your convictions. Many people find this difficult because they want to be liked by everybody. Life is not a popularity contest! If a person who makes you uncomfortable does not like you, so what? Your happiness and well-being are far more impor-tant than being liked by unlikable individuals.

5. *Hands Off.* If a coworker or boss lays a hand on you anywhere you do not want him/her to, face him/her directly, look him/her in the eye, take his/her hand off you, and say clearly and loudly, "Take your hands off me. I don't like that." Again, if he/she says, "Boy, are you the sensitive one," or "I was only being affectionate," reply with, "Whatever you think of it, I don't like being touched. Don't do it again." Document and report the incident if appropriate.

If someone presses his/her body against yours, immediately shove it away strongly, look the aggressor directly in the eye, and say loudly, "Don't do that. I don't like it." Document and report.

6. *Show and Tell.* Sometimes, a coworker will do something that could be innocuous, but you are uncomfortable with it. For example, if you feel uncomfortable when a boss shows off his/her weight loss by pulling out the waistband of his/her slacks, respond by loudly and vocally sharing this with other coworkers ("Show and Tell"): "Bill, Patty, see how much weight the boss has lost, isn't that great!" Similarly, if a coworker suggests you get together for a drink after work and you're uncomfortable with the offer, you can respond by saying: "What a great idea, I think we should all go out together; let me see what Mary and Tom are doing later." This kind of response diffuses a potentially private and unwanted intimate encounter and makes it an innocent social event.

In both cases, if the individual really wants to show off a weight loss or have some company to wind down with after work, including other people will be fine. If the person wants to get you in a sexual or potentially sexual situation, he/she will be put off by the publicness of the situation and will be unlikely to pursue things further with you. If the harasser does not give up, be more direct. Tell the harasser clearly and directly to stop his/her unwanted advances. Document and report.

7. *Keep the Baby, Throw Out the Bath Water.* Sometimes a situation is ambiguous. For example, a boss may want to talk to you about a promotion, but suggests meeting after hours to do so. You are uncom-

fortable with meeting your boss after work, but most certainly want to discuss a possible promotion. Rather than dismissing the entire situation as unwanted, keep what is worthwhile by responding positively to what is appropriate, in this case, discussing the promotion ("keep the baby"), and changing what is inappropriate ("throw out the bath water"), in this case, the after-hours' meeting: "Yes, I'm very interested in discussing a promotion, and I'm available anytime between 9:00 and 5:00 here at the office."

Either your boss will get the hint and respect your preferences, or he/she will not, in which case the situation is no longer ambiguous. You can then deal with it as an out-and-out sexual-harassment situation.

Conclusion. You are a valuable person. You have the right to live your life free of sexual harassment. Respect that right and use the preceding techniques to help others respect it as well.

> *I'm stirred when someone says, "You can do it." I find the statement "You can't" offensive to the human spirit. We can be anything. Maybe this entire experience is a series of lessons to learn that you can—yes, you can.*
>
> MAYA ANGELOU

Seducers

You're at a party. Some stranger walks up to you and he starts flirting with you, big time. He's so gorgeous and charming, you keep looking behind you, thinking he must have you mistaken with somebody else, this type of person is never attracted to you, and yet there is no mistake. He is most definitely flirting with you. He's behaving as if he knows you, creating a sort of "us" out of the two of you, standing there chatting in the middle of the room. He takes an appetizer off a plate and says, "Here, you must try this," and feeds it to you so sensuously, you think you're going to faint. A little later he says, "Let's get out of here," and even though there's a warning going somewhere in the back of your brain yelling "Danger! Danger!" off you go, little lamb led to slaughter, with a perfect stranger you've known for all of 20 minutes. . . .

The next few days are perfect bliss, as the two of you spend more time in a bed than you ever thought possible. Who knew you need only a couple of hours of sleep a night? The fact that your lover wants to stay in the bedroom morning, noon, and night and never go anywhere else doesn't bother you a bit. You feel vibrant and whole, as if somehow everything is right with the world. You want to scream out to everyone you know, "I'm in love, I'm in love, I'm in love!" And the fact that your lover wants to keep the two of you a "secret" only adds to the romance and the excitement of it all.

Until a few days or weeks later when your lover either fails to show up (permanently), or announces "It's been real" and dumps you, or you find out he is bedding someone (or a lot of someones) else at the same time as you, at which point you remember that "Danger!" warning that you were only too happy to ignore before.

You feel like such a fool! Now, of course, you see your lover in the cold light of having been dumped/abandoned/betrayed. You see that you were simply used to bolster your lover's ego or to provide sex, money, whatever it was he took from you, and that there was no relationship there. There was only using. The thought is hardly comforting.

So what happened? Just because you feel like a fool doesn't mean you are one. And you know you're not. You simply got caught up in the fantasy so cleverly woven by your lover and confused it with reality.

Seducers (for that is what your lover was) prey on our desire to be loved, cherished, valued, made to feel special. So much of what goes on in our lives doesn't make us feel special. You do your job, you take care of what has to be taken care of, you go about the daily business of living—and where in this does someone ever say "Wow! You're a terrific human being, I hang on your every word, your every look, your every gesture. I think everything you are and do is fantastic." Probably never. And yet we crave it and are willing to put up with the most horrendous relationships trying to get it. Seducers take advantage of that vulnerability and deliberately use it to get what they need—power and control over another human being. Or what they mistake for such.

So what do you do? Avoid all good-looking individuals who flirt with you? Of course not! What a dull existence that would be. What you do is:

1. *Don't buy into the assumption of "instant intimacy."* You are not a "we" or "us" with someone you've just met. Beware of individuals who create a false sense of "together" too rapidly.

2. *Listen to your own "Danger!" warnings.* Most of us recall, in hindsight, hearing that warning but ignoring it. Don't ignore it!

165

3. *Beware of individuals who don't want to be seen in public with you or who want secrecy of some sort.* In all likelihood they have something to hide. Secrecy may feel romantic, but it almost always is just a front for wrongdoing.

4. *Take the time (months, not weeks) to get to know someone before you give him/her your heart or see him/her as the answer to your prayers.* If he/she is, the person will still be there in the long run.

Hearts are not had as a gift, but hearts are earned.

WILLIAM BUTLER YEATS

The Seduction of Blame

There you are, lying flat on your back underneath the kitchen sink, trying valiantly to repair the plumbing as it drips cold water all over your face, and you cry out to your mate/child/roommate, "Would you hand me the wrench, please?" and he nonchalantly ambles over, munching on a chip, and asks, "What wrench?" "The wrench" you say, exasperated. "The only wrench we have!" "Oh, that wrench," he says. "I lent it to so-and-so a couple of weeks ago." "You what!" you say, banging your head as you move too quickly out of your watery hole. You then proceed to bawl him out for a good 20 minutes, following him about the house to do so, for his stupidity in not only lending the wrench without telling you, but failing to get it back when he knew perfectly well you'd had "fix leaky plumbing" on your to-do list this week. Your blaming session evolves into an "and-not-only-that" tirade in which you remind him of all the other things you haven't been able to accomplish because of his ineptitude—meanwhile, your sink is still leaking, and you are no closer to that wrench.

Or, you have this great business idea. Some people are interested in funding it. The deal falls through. You're a mess. Your brilliant idea gone down the tubes all because these people couldn't keep their word, didn't come through for you. You grouse, you moan, you groan—and time goes by and your brilliant idea is developed by somebody else, and you blame the unfairness in the world.

Ah, the seduction of blame. Blame is an unbelievably powerful seducer. Blame can make you feel good about yourself as you rail against the people or situations that seem to prevent you from reaching your goals or doing what you want. Blame can make you feel righteous—you were doing everything right, and if everybody else would just have gone along with your program, everything would be just fine. Blame is an ego-drug, making you feel superior and better than. But in the process, blame is seducing you away from your goals, tantalizing you away from your dreams, stopping your forward progress dead in its tracks. Because while you're busy blaming, you're not out there solving the problem. And the problem doesn't just sit. It usually gets worse.

So why do we do it? Because it feels good. It's as simple as that. At the moment, it feels so ego-rewarding to be righteous, especially when you *are* right! Your mate/child/roommate shouldn't have lent the wrench without telling you; business partners should keep their word. But meanwhile, the plumbing isn't fixed and your deal isn't getting financed. What to do? How do you avoid the seduction of blame?

1. *Accept the new situation.* You don't have a wrench. Accept it. Why you don't have a wrench and whose fault it is is irrelevant at the moment. Tell your ego to stay out of it. Send your mate out for a wrench or go get one.

Your business deal fell through. Accept it. Without losing a beat, seek new financing, draw up contracts in a different way (learning from the failed situation) so that there is less opportunity for people to go back on their word.

2. *If it is appropriate (if you intend to have an ongoing relationship with the person), deal with the person's failure to play his part as a new and different problem to solve, NOT as an opportunity to blame.* In other words, once the leaky plumbing is fixed, discuss the situation with your mate/child/roommate. "Not having a wrench made it difficult for me to get the plumbing fixed. How can we work it out so this sort of thing

doesn't happen again? What can we do here?" Your ego won't be so glo-rified, but chances are you will work successfully through the problem and come to a new understanding with your mate/child/roommate. And if you don't intend to have an ongoing relationship with the person involved, there is no need to revisit the problem with him.

Your goals (big or small), your dreams, your desires are too important to let blaming others stand in the way of your accomplishments. Don't let a greedy ego suck the life out of your dreams.

> *Obstacles don't have to stop you. If you run into a wall, don't turn around and give up. Figure out how to climb it, go through it, or work around it.*
>
> MICHAEL JORDAN

The Problem with Control

The interview is important to you. It was hard to get, and you want everything to go smoothly. You know the traffic can be bad, so you allow plenty of time to get there. But then your worst nightmare happens. The bus is late or your car won't start, there's a major accident and the traffic is tied up for miles. Despite your good intentions, despite your allowing plenty of time, you're going to be late—very late. You scream out, "Why does this always happen to me! Why can't anything go my way?!"

Your spouse likes peace and quiet when he comes home at night. So do you. Your 11- and 15-year-olds fight all the time. You know this. You know your spouse is going through a particularly bad time at work and it's important that the kids toe the line. You tell them clearly the consequences for acting up that evening. The kids know you're serious, because you do follow up with the consequences. But this night, despite your best efforts at controlling your kids' outbursts, no sooner has your spouse walked in the door than the kids start hollering, slamming doors, and raising a horrible ruckus, whereupon your spouse glares at you and demands, "Can't you control those brats for just one evening? Just a few hours? Is that too much to ask?"

It's no better at work. You try to get projects done on time—and someone or something prevents that from happening. You're so tired of trying to hold it all together, you could cry. You're ready to either punch someone's lights out or plain old give up. It seems no matter how hard you try, you can't control a darn thing.

And you're right, you can't. "Oh, well, fat help you are, Dr. Noelle," you say. "I already knew that, so what the heck am I supposed to do about it?" Quit trying to control. "What, give up?" you ask. "Throw in the towel? Let my world go to heck in a handbasket?" No. *Quit trying to control.* Instead, learn to *respond.*

You see, control demands that others behave in set, predictable ways. Whether it's the traffic, your kids, your coworkers, or your employees, none of these are going to behave completely predictably. Certainly, much of the time you can predict situations and behavior, but many times you can't. And it's those times you can't when you need another approach.

When you're in control mode, your first impulse when something goes out of control is to say, "What happened here? Whose fault is it? Get back on track!" which will work if you have power of life and death over the situation, but that's rarely the case. Let's face it, the traffic doesn't care about you; your kids can be coerced into submission, but you'll then be dealing with increasingly resentful kids; and your coworkers are not about to put up with you as Commander Supreme.

"But if I can't control, what do I do?" you cry out, feeling helpless and frustrated. You respond.

1. *Start by acknowledging that the situation is out of control.* Stop trying to control.

2. *Focus on finding a solution rather than pointing fingers.* For now, don't concern yourself with "Who did it?" Instead, concern yourself with "How can I resolve this?" Use your imagination and creativity. You have plenty of time later to sort out responsibility and accountability.

3. *Start dealing with the situation immediately.* OK, the traffic is hideous. Call your interviewer, for example, now, as soon as you see the situation, and tell him what's up. Then ask him, "What's your prefer-

ence here? Shall we reschedule the interview or what?" In the second situation, your kids are being horrible. As soon as they start, put them in separate rooms immediately, call a time out. Don't get involved in "He started it, she started it." Same thing with your coworkers. Don't look for who did what to whom. Concern yourself with "We're having trouble getting this work in on time. What's in the way? What can we do here?" Listen, negotiate, be eager to help.

Control can feel great. You snap your fingers and people jump. The only problem is, it rarely works for any length of time and almost never when the unexpected happens. You'll get much further ahead giving up on control, rather than giving up on the situation.

> *See everything. Overlook a great deal. Improve a little.*
>
> POPE JOHN XXIII

What, Little Ol' Me?

You go about your job, just one of the many people in the work world. You go to the gym, and once again, you are but one of many people. You stand in line at the bank, and indeed, you are just one of many people. Driving in your car, doing errands, going about the living of your life, it seems you are just one of—many.

You try to be a good person, but you wonder, "Why bother? What difference can I make? I'm not a celebrity, a politician, or a millionaire. How could whatever I do matter when I'm just this tiny speck in the huge mass of people on the planet?" And you get discouraged, especially when it seems the good guys are hardly making a dent, while the bad guys keep destroying all that is good. And you forget, you forget how tremendously important you are in the grand scheme of things, how every one of your kind gestures, every one of your good deeds, ripples like a pebble tossed in a pond, to the farthest reach of the planet. You forget—your impact.

You have impact. Whether you realize it or not, whether you do it consciously or not, whether you believe it or not, you have impact. Everything you say or do impacts other human beings and the world we live in. "Oh, sure," you say, "I know I have impact on my friends, my family, my dog, but come on, surely I don't have impact on the guy in the street; he doesn't even know me! Maybe in some grand philosophical sense, some foo-foo New-Age way I have impact, but day to day," you scoff, "please, give it a rest."

Ah, but that is where you are so mistaken. Day to day is where you have tremendous impact. You just aren't aware of it. "Right," you say, shaking your head at my obvious insanity, "prove it." I take you up on your challenge. Let's take that guy in the street. He's carrying a bunch of cartons or papers; he drops something. You pick it up, hand it to him with a slight smile, then just turn and go along your way. He's surprised. Usually he has to stop, put down his load, and rejuggle everything, which makes him late and puts him in an anxious, unhappy frame of mind. Because of your kind gesture, he can just continue along his path, without worrying about being late. His spirits are lifted because, gosh, there is actually one nice person on the planet. And that someone did something nice for him. Wow. He goes to his appointment feeling good about the world. His meeting goes well because of it. The person he's meeting with is the recipient of his good mood. That person is uplifted by the meeting going well, and goes about his day feeling more positive. Their positivity then impacts their interactions with the people in their world, and so it goes, on and on.

You have impact. You matter. You are important. It isn't your station in life that makes you important, it isn't how much money you make or how famous you are or anything else like that—it's YOU. If you seek to have positive impact in your world, status, money, and such certainly can increase that impact, but the bottom line is—good people have positive impact, destructive people have negative impact, be that with one person or a million. And the impact you have on one person does ripple out to a million. So whichever way you look at it, from being "just one of many" or being a celebrity/politician/millionaire— your impact is felt by millions. "Wow," you say, "I never thought of it that way." Most people don't. They forget how wonderfully important they are, how critical each and every one of us is to the happiness on this planet. Do one nice thing for one person, one tree, one animal every day of your life, and the world changes. "But that doesn't always

174

happen," you say. "Sometimes the guy just accepts your picking up his dropped carton and continues on in a nasty mood. Some people are just negative people." True. But even if your kind gesture has positive impact just one time out of ten, think of the difference it makes.

You matter, you are important, you have impact. Let that impact matter. Take it to heart. Be aware of it. And change the world.

Little things don't mean a lot—they mean everything.

HARVEY MacKay

Challenging "It's OK"

You're going along in your job, and it's OK. Not a wonderful job, not a terrible job, just a job. Pays the rent, puts food on the table. It's OK. You grouse a fair amount about it, complain about your boss, the hours, your salary, the commute, but hey—it's a job. It's OK.

You're going along in your relationship, and it's OK. Not a great relationship, not a terrible relationship, but then, whose is? You have someone to go to the movies with, someone to share your bed with, it's OK. You grouse a fair amount about it, complain about his bad habits, what you have to do to keep him happy, the lack of meaningful conversation, passion, genuine growth, but hey—it's a relationship. It's OK.

Except . . . that a job, your relationship, the different things that make up your life, these ARE your life, and often when seen in that light, "OK" isn't really "OK."

You see, sometimes what's going on is this: "This job/relationship/whatever is OK *for now*. I'm handling as much as I want to right now, and even though I recognize this isn't what I want forever, I'm content to let it be this way for now." That's fine. You're aware of what you're doing. You have made a conscious decision to let things be for the moment. But most of the time, for too many of us, what's going on is this: "I'm too busy/preoccupied/lazy to really take stock of whether or not what is going on with my job/relationship is truly 'OK' with me.

Maybe I'm too afraid of what I'll find if I look. Maybe I can't do any better than this, maybe I don't have what it takes. Maybe I like grousing better than changing, because change scares me half to death. Maybe I can't admit any of this to myself. So I'll make unhappy noises, but I'll stay with what I've got." And all that stays buried somewhere in your unconscious, while you muddle through life with things just being "OK."

Revolt! Rebel! Stand up for yourself! You deserve better than "OK." *This is your life!* Why spend it just making do? And rather than spin your wheels blaming your current condition (job/relationship/whatever) on the state of the nation, your parents' pathetic way of raising you, or some imagined flaw in your person—rise to the occasion!

Ask yourself a key question: *"Where is this leading me?"* It doesn't matter if you're looking at a work choice, a mate, or a behavior of yours, the question is the same: "Where is this leading me?" For example, if your job is unsatisfactory in all respects, then staying there is leading to your never having the financial means you aspire to, never having a sense of contributing productively to the world, never having a challenging and interesting relationship with coworkers or employer. Get real with yourself. If that is truly OK with you, then fine! Now at least you've made a consciously aware decision, and you can live with that decision. But if it isn't, move on.

If your relationship is ho-hum, filled with meaningless silences, boring conversations, a clinging just out of fear of loneliness, ask yourself, "Where is this leading me?" Clearly to an unfulfilled and unfulfilling relationship life. Again, get real. If this is truly what you want, fine. Then quit complaining! But if it's not, move on. Either move on in the sense of radically changing your own way of behaving within the relationship so the relationship becomes a more satisfying one, or move on in the literal sense of ending the current relationship and seeking a different partner.

The deceptively simple question, *"Where is this leading me?"* can be a profound life-changer. However many lives we may have, we are aware only of the one we are currently living. So make the best of it. Don't accept "It's OK" when you don't mean it. Challenge yourself to have the most fulfilling, happy, loving life you can create for yourself. It is life's best reward.

> *We either make ourselves miserable, or we make ourselves strong. The amount of work is the same.*
>
> CARLOS CASTANEDA

Holiday Blues

Life doesn't respect the holidays. When difficult things happen around the holidays we feel particularly vulnerable. Your marriage falls apart, you get fired, that promotion you counted on doesn't come through, you get dumped by the one person you thought would be there forever . . . somehow all of this is worse when it happens right around the holidays.

"I'm right back where I started from!" you moan. "No job, no relationship—I'm broke and all alone, how awful! Everybody around me has money to spend for the holidays, a loved one to spend them with, everyone except me." And indeed, it does feel awful. Certainly if you define your current situation as one of "right back where I started from," seeing everyone happy and content but yourself, it can feel horrible.

There is another perspective, however. There is another way to look at your woes and miseries. The holidays, regardless of which holidays you celebrate, are both a time of rejoicing and a time of beginning. The New Year marks the passage of the old, the "been there, done that," and welcomes the new. What is the new? The untried, the untested, the potential, the hopeful, the *possible*.

For every end, there is a beginning. For all that you are in pain over the death of your marriage/your job, the unceremonious dumping by your loved one/your boss, that is the past. No matter how lovely or beautiful the relationship/situation, it's over. No matter how ugly or painful the relationship/situation, it's over. The holidays can help remind you that the new is just around the corner. Even as we celebrate the end of the year, we turn to welcome the *New* Year.

You are never "right back where I started from." It may feel that way, and your alone/penniless situation may look that way, but the truth is, you change with every minute that passes. If you choose to, you can learn from everything that happens to you. You have now the benefit of the *experience* of your situation. You can look at what happened and learn from it. Perhaps you got involved with your job or your loved one before realizing fully what she was like, what being involved with her would require of you. Perhaps what was required wasn't comfortable, or natural, or even possible for you. Perhaps you didn't have the skills to be successful in this particular relationship or job. Whatever the case, you're not "back to where I started from." You are richer by far from your experience, as you are willing to learn from it and incorporate what you learn.

Even as you downsize your living situation to accommodate your being fired or the lack of promotion, for example, let that be the end of the old. As soon as you can, turn your attention to the new. Let this be an opportunity to review your working situation and see: "Is this really what I want to be doing with my life? What new possibilities, what new potential would I like to explore?"

Use the holidays as you would a cocoon. Reach out to your friends, support groups, minister/rabbi/priest, family, whoever is willing to give you a hand, and wrap yourself in that love and support. Use the holidays to remind yourself of the love that does exist all around us all the time, if only we would reach out to it. Use the holidays as a time of transition. Gnash your teeth, weep your tears, grieve what was, and then turn resolutely toward the new.

Let the holidays work for you, rather than turning them against you. Soak up the feelings of good will, peace, and brotherhood that tend to be more prevalent at this time of year, let them fill you with hope for the new, and be about the living of your life, seeking the joy that is rightfully yours all year 'round.

> *There is no medicine like hope, no incentive so great, and no tonic so powerful as expectation of something better tomorrow.*
>
> ORISON SWETT MARDEN

The Fulfillment of Giving

Work has become an absolute drag. It's all you can do to force yourself through the motions. You get in late, clock out early, make lunch last as long as possible, and take every single break you can possibly get away with. Nothing terrible has happened. Your job hasn't changed much, you just hate it, pure and simple. When I ask you why, you cry out, "All this job does is take from me! Take my skill, my time, my energy, I hate it!" When I ask why you continue to do it, you reply, "To take home a paycheck, of course."

Or . . . being a mom/dad is absolute hell. Your teenager is driving you right through the roof, your ten-year-old is in full manic-energy mode (without even the excuse of a psychiatric disorder), and you would give anything to sell them off to the first willing soul, although of course you'd never do that (the guilt would overwhelm you) but . . . it is tempting. And when I ask you why, you cry out, "All these children do is take from me! Take my efforts, my time, my energy. I hate it!" When I ask why you continue to do it, you reply, looking at me very strangely, "Well, I have to take care of them, don't I? I'm their mother/father."

Two very different situations, yet the same cry. Two very different situations, yet the same problem. Taking.

Taking implies something given unwillingly. It is something you didn't want to give to that situation or person. When someone or something takes from you, quite naturally you feel resentful.

What may be less obvious is that when you take from another, instead of receiving from him or her, it isn't rewarding. Oh, short-term, taking may seem very rewarding. Taking money from someone who doesn't want to give it to you may fatten your wallet, and that may feel good at the moment, but to people with a conscience, knowing you've taken something from someone who wasn't happy to give it rarely makes you feel good in the long run. Vindicated, perhaps, but happy— probably not.

"So fine, I'm not happy," you say. "I knew that already. What am I supposed to do about it, put on a happy face in front of the boss/kids and pretend I'm happy?" No. That wouldn't work, for them or for you. Instead, look into what you can *give* to the job, to the kids, and what you can *receive* from each of them.

1. *Give.* Giving is a choice. Giving always implies free will. "I'm already giving, I'm giving until I'm bleeding," you cry out. No you're not. You're allowing the job, for example, to take from you; you're not giving anything to it. Giving of yourself to your job would mean asking yourself, "What can I give of myself, where can I find room for self-expression in this job? How creative can I be in how I approach this job? How can I do my job in a way that brings me and others pleasure?" In other words, stop expecting the job to fulfill you and start giving to it so that the dynamic of job-with-me-giving-to-it fulfills you.

Being the mom/dad, ask yourself, "What am I willing to freely and graciously give to my children? What boundaries do I need to set so I'm giving graciously and not resenting every moment with them? How can I restructure the way our family functions so I am able to give and feel good about it, not be constantly and continuously taken from?"

2. *Receive.* When you give to your job, you can receive your paycheck with joy, feeling deserving and valued. You can appreciate the acknowledgment of service well done your paycheck represents. When you give graciously to your children, you can receive their affection

with pleasure. Heck, you can maybe actually see their attempts to please you (and therefore receive from them), now that you're not focused on how much they take from you.

When it comes to fulfillment, giving and receiving will always win out. Work with those areas of your life that bring you less than the joy you deserve, find ways to give to and receive from them, and watch your happiness quotient soar.

> *The measure of mental health is the disposition to find good everywhere.*
>
> RALPH WALDO EMERSON

A Question of Character

There has been much talk lately about character, be that in connection with the White House or on other political fronts. "Yes, I know, I know," you say, "that's all we hear about, so-and-so has character, so-and-so doesn't. So what?! And what does that have to do with me?" A lot, actually. For character, you see, is the basis for trustworthiness—yours and that of the people in your life. When someone with character says they will do something, you can rely on her word. When someone who lacks character says he will do something, maybe he will and maybe he won't. It's not necessarily that he is flaky, he may simply not have developed the muscle that is character.

So your current flame says he will be faithful to you only, and you find him in bed with another. Betrayal! Pain! And your lover says, "It was nothing, just a physical thing, you're the only one who matters, I didn't mean to hurt you," and indeed all that may be true, but the bottom line is you relied on him to be faithful to you, but your lover, lacking character, wasn't.

Your boss promises you that raise, that promotion, if only you'll please put in more unpaid overtime, be a part of the "team," forget about your personal life. You go along, relying on the boss's word. The only raise you get is in the number of projects and duties you have to handle, and when you remind your boss of her promise, all you get is, "Negative cash flow, sorry, just hang in there, as soon as things turn around, you're at the top of the list." Your boss has character, all right, but you've not understood it.

"OK, OK," you exclaim, "I got it, character is important. But what exactly is it?" Character is the ability to behave according to principles that reflect your values. If you have a value of honesty, for example, you hold honesty as important, something to live up to. You have principles that reflect that value in your everyday life; you won't lie, you won't steal, you don't try to do the least work possible to "get by" at your job. Character is the degree to which you actually behave in accordance with your principles.

"Great!" you say despondently. "So how the heck am I supposed to know if someone has character, or if I've misunderstood the person's character before he actually breaks his promises to me?"

By observation. Don't take for granted that a person is able or willing to follow through on her promises to you. Pay attention. Look first to what a person's values are. If your boss's sole value is profit, then her principles will reflect that. "Anything to make a buck" is likely to be your boss's guiding principle. Your boss may have tremendous character—meaning she will behave in line with that principle and value profit—which leaves your raise out in the cold, but does make your boss totally reliable. You can rely on your boss to do "anything to make a buck." And that does make her completely trustworthy—not to her promise to you, but to her overriding value.

Your lover may want to be faithful, but really has only a vague sense of "life is to be enjoyed" as his value and a generic "have fun" as his principle. Your lover lacks character because he lacks a grounded sense of values and principles. Your lover won't be trustworthy in any number of situations, because lacking values and principles, he has nothing with which to guide behavior.

So, what to do? Start with yourself. Figure out what is important to you, what you value, and think about the principles you could use to guide your behavior. For example, let's say you value respect. You think it's important to respect people. One of the principles you develop is, "Listen to people when they speak to you"; another is, "Be prompt, respect other people's time." Then develop the muscle of character, practice listening to people, practice being prompt. Little by little you will become a person of character, and in the process you will become more attuned to other people of character. Soon you will find your life is filled with trustworthy people, and what a nice life that will be.

You must look into people, as well as at them.

LORD CHESTERFIELD

A Matter of Balance

You are not a moaner or a groaner, no way, not you. You pride yourself on being compassionate, understanding of other people's difficulties, and you tolerate life's various frustrations well. So it's totally in
character for you to pretty much ignore your girlfriend's annoying
behaviors, your coworker's pettiness, and your friend's criticalness.
When you get that bleeding ulcer, the doctor asks you, "Any unusual
stressful situations in your life?" and you automatically say "No." After
all, you've not been fired, you're not in the midst of a relationship crisis, and your car is actually running. It never occurs to you that the way
you handle your girlfriend's annoying behaviors, your coworker's pettiness, and your friend's criticalness has anything to do with the state of
your health. . . .

Or, you've been working on a super-important project for the last
three months. It's been push-push-push, nonstop. You've barely slept,
eaten on the run, not gotten any exercise, and your family? Who are
they? And then, wham, in the middle of this—you get a cold. "Oh, no!"
you croak, your voice reduced to bullfrog status. "I need this like a hole
in the head! I can't afford to be sick, not now!"

Actually, you can't afford NOT to be sick. Your body is reacting
to your incredible work load by getting sick, not to punish you, but to
warn you that such a work load is self-destructive. Your body is trying
to be nice to you. And if you insist on ignoring its message, masking
your symptoms with various drugs just to get you through another day,

eventually your body will generate something much more incapacitating—pneumonia, say, or severe bronchitis.

Sophisticated city dwellers that we are—linked, connected, and wired to virtually everyone and everything—we tend to forget that our bodies, those marvelously nontechnological, touchy-feely fleshy vehicles we use and abuse are what is most closely linked and connected to us. Body/mind is a wholistic system. One invariably impacts and responds to the other. And mind isn't just your brains. Mind is your brains, your heart (emotions), and your soul. Brains, heart, soul, and body all work together to help you survive and thrive. There is a wonderful balance among all the parts of your being that, when respected, provides you with the energy, strength, and mental/emotional/spiritual well-being to rise to the challenges of living. When you get out of balance, a part of you will try to get through to you with a warning: "Hey, pay attention here! You're in trouble."

It's great to be tolerant and let a lot of life's minor irritations roll off you without paying them much heed, but it's important also to let people know how you feel about such irritations. Let your girlfriend know it's uncomfortable for you when she is always late, or leaves her clothes lying about. Talk calmly and considerately about such matters and try to resolve them. It may not seem like much, but the accumulation of little annoyances, unexpressed, does throw your body/mind system off balance and can lead to physical ailments. Once again, your body isn't trying to hurt you, it's trying to get you to deal with those annoyances so you don't have to continue to have a painful ulcer. Failure to deal with painful or uncomfortable emotions can frequently lead the body to respond in a way that will get your attention, so it's hoped you will deal with those emotions. Scientists are fully aware, for example, of the connection between repressed anger and cancer.

Rather than wait until your body has to speak up on your behalf, act now! *Become more aware* of when you are out of balance, whether that's because you are running your body ragged to satisfy the demands of work or denying your emotional reality in the name of "peace" or forgetting your spiritual connection because, "Who needs that stuff anyway—where's God/Goddess when it's time to pay the rent?" or letting your body appetites rule your life, ignoring the messages of your emotions and brains.

Pay attention to how you live your life and ask yourself periodically, "Am I in balance? Am I paying attention to what the different parts of my being are telling me?" A little awareness will go a long way in helping you live the full and rich life you deserve.

> O*ne half of the troubles in the world can be traced to saying "yes" too quickly and not saying "no" soon enough.*
>
> JOSH BILLINGS

When Agendas Collide

Your 15-year-old spends hours on the phone speaking to her friends, ties up your computer for long stretches of time writing e-mails to the same friends she just spoke with, and then is incensed when you have the audacity to ask her to please finish her chores before she goes out to spend time "hanging out" with those same friends. "Mom!" she wails, "you are soooooo unfair! You never want me to spend any time with my friends!" Still trying to live up to TV's rendition of the understanding parent, you point out that you're asking for only ten minutes of her time and that she just spent four hours of her time with friends on various communication devices. "You don't understand anything," she cries out, "these are my friends. I have to see them!" checking her pager, which has beeped at least three times in the last five minutes. "See, they're calling me, they need me!" "Well, I need you too," you say, exasperated and out of patience. "It'll take you less time to just finish your chores than to stand there and argue with me about them." "Oh, fine," your daughter practically spits the words out. "Fine, if that's the way you want it," and off she stomps, banging doors, muttering insults and threats of doom as she goes about the unbelievably tedious tasks of making her bed and cleaning up the kitty litter.

You sigh. Whatever happened to that innocent and lovely child who used to *want* to help you? Who took pleasure in just being around you and pitching in whenever you asked? Your son is no different. He's just more sullen than screamy, but it's the same battle. So what do you do? Wait for them to grow up and come to their senses? That would be fine, except you have to survive the growing-up part.

Instead, what might be helpful is for you to start by recognizing that you and your teenagers have very different agendas. Teenagers' primary focus is their peers. Developmentally speaking, teenagers are sorting out their identity—who they are—and as your teens are going about the confusing task of figuring out who they are, the one thing your teens are most emphatically sure of is—they don't want to be you. Everything else in their identity may be up for grabs, but this part is certain. Your teenagers may occasionally look to a "cool" adult as a role model, but their steady day-in day-out diet of who they look to for direction in life is their peer group. Their agenda is to be as much like, and spend as much time as possible with, their friends and to be as little like, and spend as little time as humanly possible with, you.

Meanwhile, all you're trying to do is get the chores done. And maybe help your child learn a little about responsibility in the process. In other words, teach her how to function more like an adult. Could anything be further away from your teen's desires? Learn from an adult to act like an adult? Horrors!

Clearly, you have two different agendas. How do you deal with this? First of all, by *acknowledging,* both to yourself and to your child, that there are two different agendas operating here. "I know your friends are very important to you and that you want to spend as much time as possible with them, and that's fine, I respect that," you say, acknowledging your teen's agenda. Then acknowledge your own: "What's important to me is to have all of us participate in taking care of ourselves and our home, and I'd like you to respect that." Your teen will probably respond with something mildly sarcastic like, "Fine, whatever," but the groundwork has been laid. You're no longer arguing about whose agenda is right. Now you can get on to the *negotiating* or *directing* phase. "Please do your chores quickly now so you can be with your friends as soon as possible" is very directive, yet there is an implied negotiation: "Do what I ask and you can have what you want." Notice I did not use the word "but" anywhere in the communication. When you use the word "but," as in: "That is important to you, *but* this is important to me," people's response is frequently an automatic knee-jerk defensiveness.

Parenting is, without question, the most difficult job in the world. Recognizing the different agendas you and your child may have is one way to make it a little bit easier.

> *T*he best way to make children good is to make them happy.
>
> OSCAR WILDE

On Addiction

I was recently invited to participate in a *Montel Williams Show* entitled "Teenage Girls Addicted to Sex." Despite the sensationalistic-sounding title, Montel's emphasis was on how we can help our young people heal from such addictions, not on lurid descriptions of "Who-did-what-to-whom-and-in-what-position," and the show was downright inspiring.

"That's nice, Dr. Noelle," you say, "but what does this have to do with me?" "Good question," I reply, "a lot, actually." You see, one of the things that occurred to me as I interacted with these girls was the damaging impact of the label "sex addict," *when that label becomes the primary way someone defines him-/herself.* And that's where what these girls experience can be of benefit to many of us.

Lots of us have suffered from an addiction of one type or another, addiction being defined in general terms* as using something to a degree where any positive effects are outweighed by negative effects, where the duration or amount of use is greater than you intend, and where you repeatedly try unsuccessfully to control or reduce your use of whatever it is. Common addictions are to caffeine, cigarettes, drugs, alcohol, certain types of food, food itself, shopping, gambling, thrill-seeking, jogging, TV watching, Internet surfing, to name but a few.

---

*Not to be understood as a complete or clinical definition of addiction.

It is, as anyone who has dealt with an addiction of any kind knows, tremendously important to recognize that, yes indeed, you are afflicted with that addiction. You cannot even begin to heal if you deny that you are at sufferance from something and are willing to face it head-on. This is the basis for the wonderful success of many 12-step programs. However, it is very damaging to start to think of yourself *primarily* as "an alcoholic," a "gambling addict," a "shopaholic," or, in the case of the teenaged girls, a "sex addict." When you do that you deny yourself the strength, force, and energy of the other portions of your being, those that are well functioning. You cease to view yourself as a whole person and start thinking of yourself, treating yourself as, and basing your entire identity on this single isolated aspect of your being, your addiction. Such a self-evaluation inevitably leads to depression, poor self-esteem, and makes recovery that much more difficult.

Your identity determines how you respond to and interact with your life. For example, if you think of yourself as a "winner," you're likely to interact and respond proactively and positively to events and people. If you think of yourself as a "loser," you're likely to be reactive and negative in your approach to life and others. Who you identify yourself as has a lot to do with how you live your life.

You can own your addiction without giving over your entire self to that addiction. In the case of the teenaged girls, I encouraged them to own their other attributes—their intelligence, ability to interact with animals, enjoyment of sports (for each girl it was different)—as at least equal in defining who they are as is their addiction to sex. You can say, "I am an alcoholic" and *also* say, "I am a proud Mom," "I am a giving person," "I am a good worker," or "I am a worthwhile human being." You can see the seriousness of your addictive behavior and work with 12-step programs, support groups, counseling, and/or in-patient treatments to heal it, all the while drawing on the strength and vigor the other portions of your being afford you.

Everyday Miracles

You are a whole human being, a wonderfully complex individual, with all sorts of facets to yourself. When one of those facets isn't contributing positively to your health and happiness, deal with it, absolutely. But never forget you are greater than any single portion of yourself and anchor yourself in that greater you, to give you the courage and confidence to heal. It is amazing the power you have within yourself, if you will but look to see who's really there.

> W*e all have ability. The difference is how we use it.*
>
> STEVIE WONDER

Try a Different Approach

A coach sits on the sidelines, calling out directions and instructions to his team as they run the ball all over the field: "Don't do that, don't throw long, you dummies . . . ah, how could you do that! That's so stupid, don't run without looking where you're going. . . . Don't you know anything? You don't make up your own rules as you go along, don't keep making the same mistake over and over. . . . ," and the more the team plays poorly and messes up, the harder the coach shouts the same messages over and over, exhausting himself with the effort he is putting into the team. And the coach wonders why this team he cares about so deeply doesn't seem to get it, why they're so nervous and drop the ball all the time and never seem to get anything right. But it never dawns on the coach to try a different approach.

Often, we are so caught up in our desire to see a certain result happen that we completely forget to notice the approach we're using. If your heart and soul are genuinely into whatever you're trying to accomplish and it's not happening, look at your approach, the "how" you're going about it to get the "what" that you want.

To return to our example: The coach's approach is to teach by giving the team a series of "don'ts," telling them what not to do: "Don't do that, don't throw long, don't run without looking where you're going, don't make up your own rules as you go along, don't keep making the same mistake over and over," and then reinforcing those "don'ts" with negative comments: "You dummies, how could you do that! That's so stupid, don't you know anything?" But it isn't working, because at no time does the coach tell the team what they should do. Nor does he tell them what they should *be*. Telling them they are "dummies," "stupid," and so on, doesn't tell the team what to be. So of course the team members just play worse and worse, thinking less and less of themselves.

Yet that is all too often how we work with ourselves. Just listen to your internal patter sometime. Chances are, most of what you will hear yourself saying to yourself is: "You dummy, how could you do that! You know better than that, don't do it that way!" when it would be far more effective (and more loving) to say to yourself, "Hey, try doing it X way, that's right, that'll work, I'll try—nope, didn't work, OK, I'll try Y way— ah yes, much better, I'm doing good here!"

You can't get to a positive result from a negative place. You can't browbeat yourself into any kind of lasting success. It's the wrong approach. Instead, tell yourself what you need to do, what will work, and reinforce your efforts with honest praise, or, put in the coach's terms: "Throw long! Look before you run! You're doing great!" and watch yourself catapult into happiness and success.

---

*P*erseverance is not a long race, it is many short races one after another.

WALTER ELLIOTT

The Way to Your Heart's Desire

We are all blessed with two wonderful tools to help us through this wild/exciting/frustrating/joyous journey called "Life": a head and a heart. Each has a different function: Your heart lets you know what you want, as in the phrase "your heart's desire"; your head helps you figure out how to get what you want. When you use your head and your heart together and appropriately, it all works out great. Problems arise when:

1. You use only one—your head all the time, forgetting your heart, or your heart all the time, forgetting your head.

2. You make the heart do the work of the head, and your head do the work of your heart.

Problem #1: Using only your head (or heart). You say to yourself, "I should mow the lawn. I should. I should mow the lawn now. Get out there, get the lawnmower and mow. Now." What do you think happens? Nothing. Why? Because there is no desire. There is no meaning behind the mowing, no joy, no significance. Only the heart can bring that.

But the heart can't do it alone. Use only your heart, and here's what happens. You say to yourself, "I want a beautiful lawn, I really do, gosh, I can just see it, a gorgeous green lawn . . ." Again, nothing happens. If you have only desire, and do not use your head to tell you how to get your desire, you end up feeling helpless and hopeless, longing for something you will never have. YUCK! But put the two together, and presto! You have magic: "I want a beautiful lawn, so I'll start by mowing."

OK, so mowing lawns may not be a big deal, but think what happens when we take the same process and apply it to love, work, finances? "I must work, I must." Why? Put like that, it's drudgery. You need the other (heart) half, "I want to feel productive and contribute to society, therefore I will work at something that allows me to do that." The heart's "I want to be rich, gee, I really do" is only a lifelong moan unless you hook it up with, "I want to be rich. OK, what are the steps I can take to getting there?!"

Problem #2: Letting your heart do the work of your head and your head take over the work of your heart. Don't let your heart dictate the way to do things or your head tell you what you want. Your heart says, "I hate to date." Your head says, "You have to or you'll never get a relationship." This is totally mixed-up. "Dating" is a strategy; your heart was never meant to design strategy. Meanwhile, your head is trying to tell you what you want: "You have to date or you'll never get a relationship." Since your head can't give you emotional motivation, it gives you an order, "You have to," which won't work.

Ask your heart what your desire is: "I want a relationship, and I don't want to date." Let your head figure it out from there. "OK. So as alternatives to dating, how about getting involved with a hobby or a class, where I can make friends and create a relationship that way?" When you allow your head and your heart to work harmoniously together in this way, you will find the way to "your heart's desire."

> *Every human mind is a great slumbering power until awakened by a keen desire.*
>
> EDGAR ROBERTS

Breaking the "I'm Sorry" Syndrome

Your friend calls, "I had a terrible day; the car wouldn't start, my kids are a mess, I'm so unhappy." You respond, "Oh, I'm so sorry." Your friend continues, "Nothing seems to go right, I don't know what to do." You repeat, "I'm so sorry," and she goes on. And on. You feel bad, powerless, and as if you should do something, but what?

You go home to your spouse, and it starts again: "I have such a headache." You reply, "I'm sorry, honey." "Yeah well," he continues, "it's really awful." You pipe up once again with "I'm so sorry," and once again, you feel hopeless and powerless and as if somehow it's your fault—that you should be able to fix it; you're a no-good person if you don't.

What are you apologizing for? Did you contribute to or cause the broken car/rotten kids/awful headache? Be honest with yourself. If you did contribute to the problem, then by all means, apologize. If you didn't, then don't. Take back your power. Don't apologize for something you didn't do; instead, express your feelings and offer help in a way that is appropriate and feels good to you.

For example, when your friend starts in with: "I had a terrible day (etc.) . . ." respond with an expression of your feelings, something along the lines of, "Gee, that sounds awful," and then ask specifically if there is something you can do: "Is there anything I can do to help?" Now, you are powerful! You are helping your friend work toward a solution, rather than offering your no-doubt heartfelt but ineffective "I'm sorry."

Let's take the situation one step further. What do you do if in answer to your offer of help, your friend just sighs and says, "No, I guess it'll be all right." If she says, "No," let it go. Don't force your help on someone who really wanted only a shoulder to cry on. But what do you do if she says "Yes" to your offer of help and gives you specific ways in which you can help? Well, you now have a choice. You can choose to help her out in the way she asks for, or you can choose not to. Again, without saying "I'm sorry!"

For example, your friend says, "I had a terrible day (etc.) . . ." You reply, "Gee, that sounds awful. Is there anything I can do to help?" Your friend replies, "Yes, actually, could you drive me to the market and then take me to the cleaners?" If you want to do that, fine, no problem. If you don't want to do it, however, having made an offer of help does not obligate you to helping in a way that is uncomfortable or difficult for you. Be creative! Think of a way to respond to your friend's request without putting yourself in a situation you don't really want to be in. For example, "Well, I can't do that for you, but I know X Market will deliver, and I could pick up your cleaning tomorrow after work."

As long as you stay in a problem-solving mode, you'll be effective and helpful. So break the "I'm-sorry syndrome"—and be a good friend.

A problem is a chance for you to do your best.

DUKE ELLINGTON

The Value of Intent

A man falls down onto the sidewalk by a bus stop. You hesitate a moment, then, when nobody else lifts a finger to help him, you rush over and assist the man, getting him on his feet, checking if he's OK, and dusting him off. Later in the restroom at work you notice used paper towels carelessly tossed outside the wastebasket; you pick them up and put them in the appropriate receptacle. On the way back to your work you go by a number of people, and you smile in greeting to them as you pass.

Gee, you sound like a pretty swell person. Very socially aware, doing your share to contribute to a "gentler, kinder nation." But if we dig a little deeper, here's what might appear. You don't really feel like helping the guy up off the sidewalk, but when nobody else does, you do so, not because you're concerned about the person who fell, but because you want to show the people who didn't help him up what jerks they are. You pick up the paper towels not because you enjoy pitching in, but because picking them up allows you to feel "better than," as in, "Well, at least I don't dump my litter all over the place; at least I know the right thing to do." And when you smile in greeting at those you pass, you do so, not to give them a little love in their day, but because if they don't smile back, you can feel righteous, "See, you try to be nice, and does it work? No, people are ungrateful and don't care." Your apparently loving behavior is really an opportunity for you to make others wrong and yourself right, even if only in your own mind.

Does this make you an evil, bad person? Of course not! It just makes you a person who hasn't yet matched your inner intent to your outer behavior. "So what difference does it make?" you might ask. "If I'm doing good things, what does it matter why I'm doing them?" Well, it matters because only caring intent will lead to feelings of joy and satisfaction. Doing things to prove others are "wrong" or "bad" hardens the heart. You end up bitter and resentful and eventually won't be able to get yourself even to do the outer behaviors. If you want to be socially conscious and contribute to the healing of our world, intent matters. You are part of the world; you, too, need love, joy, and satisfaction. When you give genuinely to others because you value their well-being, when you do things because you care, then you flood your own being with warmth and "good vibes" and, in giving, receive.

Take a look at your own behaviors. Be brave. Be honest. Tell yourself the truth. How much of what you do, do you do to make yourself look "right," and how much do you do out of genuine caring for yourself and others? Then, be even braver. Make conscious decisions as to those things you want to do out of true caring, and dump as many as possible of those behaviors you would do only to make yourself "right" and others "wrong."

What a relief! Now you can give what you truly have to give, and in the doing receive tenfold in love and satisfaction.

A soul without a high aim is like a ship without a rudder.

EILEEN CADDY

The Positive Power of Response

There is an ongoing debate among philosophers regarding how much control we have over the events of our lives; some say we have total control, some say that we have none at all. So far, no one has come up with a definitive answer. However, one thing is sure: Regardless of the control or lack of control we have over events, we have absolute control over our responses to those events.

Notice I did not say we have control over our reactions. A reaction is an automatic behavior you do without thinking. For example, you fall down, you say "ouch." There is virtually no thought between the event (falling) and the reaction ("ouch"). There is, however, thought between the event and your response to that event, your response being how you choose to define the event and what you decide to do (or not do) about it, given your "definition" of the event.

For example, you fall down. You have an infinite number of possible responses to that. You can check the damage, notice your knee is skinned, and respond as follows:

- "Hey, no biggie, stick on a Band-Aid and that's that."
- "Oh my gosh, I'm going to get gangrene. Where's the nearest hospital?"
- "The s.o.b. who built this sidewalk did this to me; I'll sue him."
- "My shoe must be too tight. I'll get a different pair."
- "These things always happen to me. Nothing ever goes right for me."

. . . and so on and on. You choose your response; at least you can choose your response if you are aware that you have a choice, lots of choices, in fact, and that you therefore have a great deal of influence on the impact of that event in your life. It all depends on the choice you make with your response.

Choose a response that will have a positive influence in your life. Stop and ask yourself: "How can I look at this event so I minimize its negative potential and maximize the positive potential?" Ask yourself what you can learn from your experience—about yourself, about others, about the world we live in, and ask yourself how you can put that knowledge to good use.

Consciously decide, for example, if you are laid up after an accident or a surgery, to be proactive, take the initiative, research all the possible avenues for rapid healing, and use your "down time" constructively: Catch up on your reading, write letters to friends, find a new hobby you can do while recuperating, decide to set a courageous example for others, write an article or a speech of your experience, share with others how you have coped, think about your life purpose, review your goals for the next two years, learn five new words a day, practice writing with your nondominant hand, keep a journal, learn to draw . . . and the list goes on.

Ordinary people have been known time and again to create incredibly positive benefits for themselves and others by refusing to focus on the negative portion of their experience. Learn to respond purposefully and positively to what life offers you and you will reap wonderful rewards.

Energy and persistence conquer all things.

BENJAMIN FRANKLIN

The Positive Power
of Response, Part Two

Ever notice how much time and energy you spend trying to figure out what someone else is thinking? Your boyfriend hasn't called for three days, you're worried sick, you've analyzed the last time you saw each other a hundred times, you figure that's it, it's over, you were such a stupid boob/too clingy/too assertive, you probably drove him off. And did you ever notice how often the conclusion you draw is negative?

"Oh dear, she looked at me funny, I'll bet she thinks I'm ugly." "He's late again, he's probably out flirting (or worse, he doesn't care about me at all)." "She's never at her desk, she really doesn't take the job seriously."

Whenever someone does something you didn't expect, you feel out of control. It's difficult to stay in that out-of-control place, it makes most of us very nervous. So what you do is try to reestablish some kind of control by jumping to a conclusion. Deciding that you know why your boyfriend hasn't called in three days may be painful, but it does bring back a sense of predictability and orderliness (control) to your personal universe. The conclusion you draw is most often negative because feeling out of control makes you feel insecure, which promptly activates all the other insecure feelings you have about yourself, and presto—a negative conclusion!

Feeling in control at the expense of your self-esteem isn't worth it. There is a way to feel both in control and maintain good self-esteem:

1. Be willing to live with several possible conclusions to whatever is going on.

2. Make sure at least some of those conclusions are not negative.

3. Regain control by determining your response to each of the possible conclusions, rather than by trying to pinpoint "the" correct conclusion (which is impossible anyway).

For example, your boyfriend hasn't called in three days. You come up with the following possible conclusions:

a. He's preoccupied with work and trusts your relationship is strong enough to withstand a few days of noncontact.

b. He's embarrassed about his own behavior during your last encounter and needs some time to get past that.

c. He's taking some private time to nourish himself so as to be more available for you later.

d. He's met someone new and is history.

Remain open to all of these (and whatever other conclusions you come up with). Don't try to figure out which one is "right"; regain a feeling of control by figuring out how you would like to respond to each of them. Once you know how you are going to respond, you are in control regardless of the true outcome.

You can't control things by setting them in cement. Everything changes all of the time even if only in apparently small ways; something is always bound to happen that will impact what seemed to be an absolutely fixed quantity in your world. You can, however, choose your response to things, and if that does not give you control over things, it certainly gives you an in-control high-esteem way of dealing with things.

*T*here are no shortcuts to any place worth going.

BEVERLY SILLS

The Joy of Meaningfulness

The alarm rings, you get up, you brush your teeth, you take your shower, you pack the kids/dog/cleaning in the car, you drop them off, you go to work, you do your job, you get in the car, you pick up the kids/dog/cleaning, you make dinner, you clean up, you go to bed, you sleep, the alarm rings, you get up, you brush your teeth, you take your shower, you pack the kids/dog/cleaning in the car . . . and so it goes. And one day you find you can't get out of bed, you can't do it any more, you don't even know why, you're not particularly tired or sick, nothing's wrong between you and your mate/significant other/kids/friends/boss, you just know you can't do it any more, and all you want to do is lie there and cry.

No, you're not going crazy. Yes, you may be suffering from depression, and that possibility needs to be considered, preferably with the help of a trained professional. But in all likelihood, what you are suffering from is a real and little acknowledged disease of the present times—meaninglessness.

Meaninglessness is easy to diagnose. Ask yourself, "What is it all for? The shower, the cleaning, the job, the dog, all of it—why do I do it?" If the answer comes up, "Because I have to," then you are suffering from meaninglessness. It quite frankly isn't valid, once you're past childhood, to do things because "I have to." One of your greatest freedoms as an adult is the freedom of choice. And one of the most wonderful choices you can possibly make for yourself is to choose to do whatever it is that you do with meaning.

To do something with meaning involves giving that act significance and value. For example, you set your alarm because you care about giving yourself adequate time to get ready for your day. You value yourself too much to rush and beat yourself through your morning. You brush your teeth and take your shower because you value your health, you enjoy feeling well, and you know that cleanliness contributes to good health. You pack the kids/dog/cleaning in the car and drop them off because you like contributing to others' (kids' and dog's) well-being as well as to your own (clean clothes = more likely successful social interactions). You go to work and do your job because you enjoy the good feeling of being financially responsible for yourself and of being productive, and so on.

The more you attribute significance and value to the ordinary tasks of everyday life, the more meaning your life acquires and the more good feelings and joy you can experience. Even stopping to let a pedestrian cross the street becomes less an obligation, "I have to, it's the law," and more a meaningful act, "I want to because I care about other people." *How* we do what we do can make the difference between a full and enriching life, and an empty and boring one. Deliberately seek for meaning in your every action and watch the joy in your life GROW!

I cannot believe that the inscrutable universe turns on an axis of suffering; surely the strange beauty of the world must somewhere rest on pure joy!

LOUISE BOGAN

210

Mindless Reaction/Mindful Choice

Someone cuts you off in traffic; you immediately feel angry: "Dumb jerk!" you yell out, and you carry that anger around with you. You start seeing jerkiness everywhere, and you end up having a fairly miserable afternoon. . . .

You come home after a long day, and you're barely in the door when your spouse cries out: "Why can't you ever call when you're going to be late—you've ruined dinner!" And you snap back: "Why do you have to get on my case the minute I hit the door? Like I really need to come home to this!" And you're both off and running, the beginning of an all-night harangue in the making. . . .

What's happening here? You don't think of yourself as an angry or mean person, and yet you certainly are behaving like one. You feel as if things are out of control, and you don't like that.

Well, you're right. Things are out of control. And the reason is you are reacting to the events in your life rather than responding to them. Reacting is an automatic behavior; there is no conscious thought between the event and what you do with that event. When you're simply reacting to what goes on in your life, you are out of control—you are not making conscious choices about how you want to behave, you're letting someone or something else push all your buttons, and whatever comes out is what comes out.

So the "dumb jerk" cuts you off in traffic and you get angry. You don't stop to think about the fact that the person was operating out of his own fears, insecurities, and anxieties. You don't stop to consider whether the person cut you off because he's scared that he won't get to where he needs to be when he needs to be there, or because he doesn't have the social skills that allow for smooth functioning in society. You just deliver a knee-jerk reaction of anger and stay stuck with it.

Instead, learn to respond. Feel your anger, of course, but then make a conscious choice whether you want to let that anger stick with you and infect your day or whether you would rather try to understand the motivation behind the individual's behavior, which will allow you to get off the anger (and thus not ruin the rest of your day) and will possibly lead you to a feeling of compassion.

Similarly, if your spouse cries out "dinner is ruined" in despair at your lateness, she is in all likelihood unhappy because she was looking forward to offering you something nice—a good dinner. Coming back with a knee-jerk reaction will only create havoc. If, instead, you respond to your initial feeling of frustration by taking a deep breath, then thinking for a moment, you may realize that your spouse is disappointed, and you can acknowledge that disappointment and from there work out a better understanding of dinner hours and what works in terms of phone calls and so forth.

Take charge of your life. You are not a mindless robot, fated to react automatically to events; you are an incredible creation, a being capable of conscious thought, of choice. Use that wondrous ability to make your life the joyous experience you truly deserve it to be.

The universe is change; our life is what our thoughts make it.

MARCUS AURELIUS ANTONINUS

Modesty—
A Misunderstood Virtue

People often hesitate to acknowledge their qualities, believing that acknowledging one's good points is immodest, but, in fact, not knowing or acknowledging one's qualities is the opposite of modesty. Modesty is knowing your qualities and strengths and consciously not flaunting them in someone's face. Not knowing or acknowledging your qualities is not modesty, it is an attempt to live a happy productive life without the proper tools. How painful! You wouldn't garden with your fingernails for a trowel—yet that's exactly what you do when you ignore your qualities.

Your qualities are your strengths. Your qualities are the assets you have available to you to help you achieve your goals and cope successfully with life's difficulties. For example, let's say that among your qualities are a good sense of humor, a positive outlook, nice eyes, and patience. And let's say you're having trouble getting along with someone at work. Use your specific strengths to cope with the situation: Let your positive outlook help you visualize a better work relationship in the future, let your patience help you hold onto your positivity, let your sense of humor take the sting out of the problem, let your eyes make genuine contact with the person and try to see through his meanness to the better side of his nature. If your strengths are different, your approach would be different. Let's say, for example, that you are very bright, a hard worker, and have strong hands. Then you might let your intelligence help you come up with more effective communication techniques, let your ability to work hard help you set specific goals to implement those ideas, and let your hands convey, by the way you hand things to your coworker or the way you handle equipment, that you are confident of a positive outcome. Same situation, two different ways of handling it, based on two different sets of strengths.

Your qualities exist on three different levels: mentally, emotionally/spiritually, and physically. Take a good look at each and figure out specifically what are your unique qualities. Physically, for example, ask yourself, "What do I like about my physical being? What do I consider my strong points?" What have people commented on about your physical being over the years: Do people tell you what a winsome smile you have, or how you always seem to be in great shape? Then ask: What have you always prided yourself on mentally? What have people commented on? Mental qualities are not simply a matter of IQ; mental qualities are about how you think: that is, are you detail oriented or into the overview, are you good at coming up with concepts or better at structuring practical matters? And so on. Repeat this process with the emotional/spiritual level: What do you like about yourself in this arena? Ask your friends to list your emotional assets; ask them to sum up your personality in a nutshell. What makes you a good friend?

Then think of each of these qualities as the tools you have to cope with life's challenges, and use these wonderful tools deliberately to create a better, happier life for yourself. You deserve it—go for it!

Don't fight forces; use them.

RICHARD BUCKMINSTER FULLER

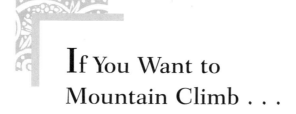

If You Want to
Mountain Climb . . .

If you are into mountain climbing, enjoy it and are expert at it, and want to go mountain climbing with a friend, pick a friend who mountain climbs. It is tragic and unfair to pick a friend who is paraplegic and afraid of heights, and expect her to mountain climb at your level of expertise. You will either spend your whole time trying to teach, cajole, push, and prod your friend into proper climbing, and/or you will be frustrated and resentful at her for not doing better and spoiling your fun. Either way, you will both have a perfectly miserable time.

This sounds like basic common sense, right? You say, "Heck, I'd never do that!" Oh yeah? Then why, when you consider yourself, for example, a "people person" and are happiest when surrounded by a lot of chatty, upbeat individuals, do you allow yourself to take a job in the back room doing accounting, where the only living thing is an occasional fly buzzing over your solitary lunch, and then groan and moan about what a horrible job you have? Why, when you're into yoga, meditation, vegetarian food, and quiet walks on the beach do you date someone who is a compulsive workaholic, who refuses to take any time off work unless it's a "networking" activity, pops Twinkies by the case, and then complain that your boyfriend is unavailable, uncommunicative, and "lacks depth"?

Respect yourself! Value who you are, what your dreams and desires are, and choose your companions and your job/career accordingly. Ask yourself: "How do I want to live my life? What are my ideals, my values, and how do I want to live these in a day-to-day fashion? What do I want for myself now—in five years—in ten years—in twenty years? How do I want to go about getting there? What are my real talents and gifts, what do I yearn most to develop in myself or to express, and how do I want to go about that?" Only when you know *what's* important to you, *where* you want to go with your life, and *how* can you realistically consider the kind of job/career and relationship that "fits" for you.

So, to go back to our examples. If you are a "people person" and want to fulfill that side of yourself, look for a job where you're sure to be surrounded by or involved with lots of chatty, upbeat individuals. If you are into yoga, etc., look for a companion who at least understands and appreciates those values, even if he does not necessarily practice them in the same way or to the extent that you do. A great deal of frustration and unhappiness in life can be avoided simply by thinking through your life choices and taking into account who you are and what you want.

In other words, if you want to mountain climb with a friend, pick a friend who mountain climbs. Then you'll be free to really develop your mountain-climbing skills, enjoy the scenery along the way, and happily share the experience with a kindred soul.

> *To be what we are, and to become what we are capable of becoming, is the only end of life.*
>
> ROBERT LOUIS STEVENSON

From "Needy" to "Deserving"

There is something really awful in the word "needy," a desperate quality from which we shy away. Unfortunately, that desperate quality also gets attached to the word "need," so that when we have a "need," as in "I need a man/woman," we immediately think, "Oh, how yucky, I need a man/woman, I must be a terrible clingy desperate creature, I shouldn't be this way, I should be self-sufficient and strong . . ." and it goes on. So when we find ourselves saying, "I need love," "I need to be held," "I need to be valued," "I need to be special to someone," more often than not we immediately discount that need, push it aside—and then we wonder why we feel so unfulfilled.

If you look up "need" in the dictionary (*Webster's New Collegiate*), however, you will find a different definition of "need": a need is defined as "a physiological or psychological requirement for the well-being of an organism." In other words, something you (the organism) require (as in "must have") to be well (feel good, be healthy, etc.). That's it. Nothing about desperation, yucky clingy stuff, or anything else shameful and embarrassing. Just a requirement for well-being.

You wouldn't for a minute even consider neglecting your cat's (or dog's or parakeet's or plant's) requirements for well-being: You appropriately water and feed and talk nice to and in general do everything you can think of to see to your pet's or plant's well-being. It doesn't occur to you to say "Well, my plant shouldn't need sun," no, you hurry up to place your plant where it will get precisely the correct amount of sun for it.

Well, what about you? Are you any less deserving of well-being than your cat/dog/parakeet/ficus? Of course not! Yet as long as you think of your needs as something you shouldn't have, you will neglect your own well-being.

Let's go back to "I need a man/woman." What does that really mean, in specifics? That you need love, affection, warmth, caring, feelings of specialness and appreciation, and that these items all contribute to your well-being. There is nothing wrong with having these as requirements for your well-being. They are very basic human requirements shared by all of us. And you deserve to have those things you require to feel good.

The first step to getting your needs met is to acknowledge your needs as wonderful requirements for your well-being and then to let yourself know that you deserve those requirements. Start by making a list of your specific needs, for example, "I need love," "I need affection," "I need caring," and then rephrase those needs into "I deserve": "I deserve to be loved," "I deserve affection," "I deserve caring." Repeat these statements out loud to yourself as often as possible and really let yourself get into the good feelings that deservability brings up, as opposed to the yucky feelings that "needy" brings up.

You cannot get what you do not feel you deserve. "I deserve" is the first step on the road to a better, happier life.

Happiness is the only good. The time to be happy is now, the place to be happy is here.

ROBERT INGERSOLL

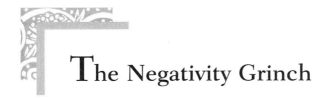

The Negativity Grinch

There is a far worse Grinch than the Grinch that stole Christmas. The Grinch that stole Christmas is but a poor second cousin compared to the real Granddaddy Grinch of them all, the Negativity Grinch.

The Negativity Grinch, when totally allowed into our hearts, can ruin the most beautiful Christmas/Hanukkah of all—the joy that is our natural birthright, whether it come from the beauty of a sunset, the glow of pride from a job well done, or the warmth of a smile. All these pale and turn cold when negativity overwhelms our lives.

Negativity, in its place, is healthful and helpful to an aware life. Negativity is what makes us ask questions, look twice at things, weigh the evidence, and take precautions in our own best interest. Negativity becomes the Negativity Grinch when it takes over the majority of your thoughts and feelings. At that point it loses its value as an "approach-with-caution" helper and turns into a "don't/can't/won't do/be anything right" hinderer. So handling negativity appropriately doesn't mean pushing all negativity out of your life forever; it means learning how to use negativity so it contributes positively to your life.

For example, the negative thought that there is violence in our world, our cities, even our own neighborhoods can either have a healthful function or an unhealthful joy-stealing one. The healthful function is that awareness of violence can motivate us to deal with and end the violence. The organization M.A.D.D. (Mothers Against Drunk Drivers) is a prime example of the healthful function of negativity. A mother whose child was killed by a drunk driver started this group, which has become a powerful lobbying force instrumental in creating new laws against drunk drivers, thereby saving many other lives. Negativity was transformed into positive good.

Allowing awareness of violence in the world to overwhelm one's thoughts and feelings, however, would have a very different effect. It would plunge you into depression and cynicism, which could lead either to inaction or random acts of destruction, neither of which are going to cure anything. The mother whose child died in the drunk-driving situation could easily have let herself be dragged down by her natural grief and concluded that life was horrible and unfair and perhaps even committed suicide as a result of her overwhelming negative thoughts and feelings. This would have been of no use to anyone and would have given the mother no joy at all. Instead, she used the negativity to motivate her to take the action that led to her healthy, positive contribution to society. Although creating M.A.D.D. could never make up for her dead child, it certainly gave her the joy of knowing she was saving many other children's lives.

Don't let the Negativity Grinch eat up your joy! Keep negativity in perspective, as a warning, a motivator, a catalyst for change, and free yourself to enjoy the sunsets, the smiles, and the love you deserve.

Those who bring sunshine to the lives of others cannot keep it from themselves.

JAMES BARRIE

What, No Guarantees?

Your still-new car is in the shop—again; your once adorable toddler is now a raving, raging adolescent; that job you thought would be yours forever has disappeared in the reconstruction of an uncertain economy; your usual good health has been replaced with some mysterious virus that has no known cure, and you dream of the "good old days" when cars ran well, children obeyed, and jobs stayed put until you left.

Dream on! Life has never had more than one guarantee (death), and clinging to the "good old days" (which if you really stop and think about it weren't all that good) is less and less possible in the face of the ever increasing pace of change. Much as we hate to face it, the bottom line is—there are no guarantees. People, cars, jobs all change. Houses fall down, fortunes are made and lost in a day, what was a hot item on the market today is good for the recycler tomorrow.

Yet all of us need safety and security. All of us need to feel that we are standing on *terra firma,* not on shifting ground. The paradox is, the more change that is happening all around us, the more we need stability.

The problem is not our need for safety and stability, the problem is where we tend to look for that safety. Looking for safety in the permanence of a job, of a person always being a certain way, of your health being everlastingly good is bound to lead to disappointment. Some if not all of these will fail you. The secret to safety and stability lies within yourself, within your ability and willingness to respond to every situation as it occurs. You see, you may not be able to guarantee a single aspect of your life, but you can absolutely guarantee your willingness to respond fully and positively to whatever comes your way. Committing to yourself in this way is what will give you the safety and stability we all require in order to live a full and satisfying life.

"OK, so fine," you say, "I'm committed to myself. But how does that help when my job has been 'merged' out of existence, or a tree just fell on my car, or my cat requires $1,000 I don't have for surgery?"

1. *Don't panic.* Breathe. Since you have a basic underlying assumption that you will respond to this situation fully and positively, know that you will do so. Affirm to yourself, "I am willing and able to respond fully and positively to this situation." Breathe again.

2. *Assess the situation.* Keep doing #1 as you write down the specifics of what has just happened and what the impact is on you: "I'm going to be without money for rent, food, etc., within two weeks." "I need to get my car fixed and get transportation in the meantime. I'm going to need money for both." "My cat will die without this surgery, she needs this surgery. Paying for it is a problem." Keep breathing . . .

3. *Brainstorm alternatives.* Most people get stuck on #2. Seeing the damage or need is overwhelming, and they can't get past that. With pad and pen, write down any and all alternative solutions that occur to you—farfetched or not. If possible, ask a close friend to help you brainstorm. Don't censor yourself. Keep coming up with ideas.

4. *Use your resources.* You are not alone. There is help all around you if only you are willing to look for it. Starting with those close to you, friends and family, think of all possible sources of help, going all the way to government and other large public-sector entities. Again, call on friends or a group of friends to help you think of all the resources available to you.

You are able to respond successfully to any situation in your life if you are willing to do so and to remember that you are not alone. Your safety is grounded within yourself—in your persistence, creativity, and willingness to call upon those resources, material and human, that are there for all of us. Now *that's* a real guarantee.

> *Responsibility is the thing people dread most of all. Yet it is the one thing in the world that develops us, gives us manhood or womanhood fiber.*
>
> FRANK CRANE

Panic vs. Problem Solving

Your employer, who may have her faults, but who generally seems appreciative of you and your work, suddenly starts finding fault with everything you do, grumbles and grouses at you no matter what the occasion, makes you do and redo work, and has you in such a tizzy you are putting in all sorts of unpaid overtime, grinding your teeth at night, and seriously thinking about getting a new job. . . .

Your husband, an ordinarily kind and loving person, starts snapping at you, complaining about this and that, responding with aggravation to just about anything you do. You panic: "Oh, my gosh, he doesn't love me anymore, that's it, he's having an affair, I've got to win him back," and off you go to buy that new outfit/lose 20 pounds/dye your hair/join a gym. All of which in and of themselves are perfectly fine things to do, and, yes, maybe they would help "the problem." But at this point, that's not what they are about; at this point, you are just wildly flailing out trying to grab onto anything that might bring you relief from the growing PANIC! you feel inside.

Panic. An awful feeling, a feeling of being out of control. A feeling that all that was right in the world is now all wrong, not understanding how it got that way—and not stopping to find out how. That's the key. Stopping to find out how things got so uncomfortable and then problem solving based on what you find out. Dealing with panic consists of being able to recognize panic for what it is—a feeling of out of control, not the reality of out of control, and then going on to problem solve.

How to do it: Don't let the feeling of panic drag you willy-nilly all over the place. Stop. Take a deep breath. Look at the reality of what is going on.

1. *Take stock of the situation.* Ask yourself, "What might be going on here? What in my behavior might be provoking such a response? What in my partner's/employer's (or child's or friend's or any other relationship) reality might generate this kind of behavior?" Be sure to look at both how you might be contributing to the situation and how the other person's reality might be contributing. Too often, when people take stock of a situation, they look only at how they contribute or look only at how the other person is contributing. Take a balanced approach. Look at both.

2. *Ask your partner/employer what's going on.* Do this without putting blame on yourself or the other: "I'm confused/I'm concerned. I've noticed that you seem to be distressed/upset a lot lately." And let him or her take it from there. More often than not, you will find that your partner's/employer's behavior has nothing to do with you. And if it does, you now have some concrete reality from which to problem solve.

You can't problem solve if you don't know what the problem is. So, stop panicking, take stock, and problem solve. It's infinitely more successful and rewarding than running around feeling powerless and out of control.

> *The future of mankind lies waiting for those who will come to understand their lives and take up their responsibilities to all living things.*
>
> VINE DELORIA, JR.

The Lost Art of Patience

There's never enough time to do everything you want to do. It does-n't seem to matter how early you set your alarm, how many time-man-agement seminars you attend, how artfully you delegate tasks to others, there's never enough time. So if someone comes along and says "Hey, be patient!" her suggestion is greeted with zero enthusiasm. Patience in the twenty-first century has come to be defined as time you waste wait-ing while you'd rather (much!) be doing something else. Which is really unfortunate, because patience is a marvelous tool.

"Great," you say, "so now you're telling me not only do I have to waste all that time waiting, I also have to like it?" No. But as you come to a truer awareness of what patience really is, you'll come to appreci-ate its value, and then, yes, you will like it.

You see, patience is the art of allowing understanding to come through the process of observation, of paying attention to detail. Because it takes time to observe thoroughly, patience is much under-rated in our fast-paced society, yet patience is a wonderful way to clar-ity and understanding—two of the most valuable skills to living successfully and happily.

You watch your child learning to tie her shoe. Patience means you observe how she goes about it, paying attention to the detail of how she attempts to coordinate fingers and lacing. Patience means you don't rush in to do it for her; instead you build her self-esteem by saying "Gee, it takes some pretty clever finger work to get those laces in those holes."

Your mate comes home ranting and raving about the traffic and "What do you mean you forgot to pick up the cleaning?" and "Oh, not meat loaf for dinner—again!" Patience means you don't defensively start in with what a horrible day you had and she's lucky you ever pick up the cleaning, and so what's wrong with meat loaf anyway? Patience means you stop a moment and observe, trying to see deeper into your mate than the surface storm and to notice her underlying distress. You set aside your feelings for the moment and say, "You had a really rough day," and that opens the door to a healing conversation for both of you.

Your heretofore good employee makes a mess of things, forgetting duties, losing messages. You don't use "patience" in the old way, waiting around to see if your employee is going to "snap out of it"; instead, you use your new definition: You pay attention to what else is going on with your employee; you observe how he is interacting with colleagues; you ask about his family, his health; you interest yourself in the details of his life; and you find out that his parent is diagnosed with cancer and is undergoing the awful side effects of chemotherapy. Your "patience" pays off. You suggest taking some vacation time/hiring a temp to give your employee shorter work hours/making yourself open to helping your employee in other ways. You help your employee get back to "exemplary-employee" status and don't damage your business in the process.

Patience is a wonderful tool. Use it lovingly and it will serve you magnificently.

The greatest power is often simple patience.

E. JOSEPH COSSMAN

Pearls Before Swine

You think you've found your true love and pour out your heart to him, do all sorts of wonderful things for him, only to have those tender confidences thrown back in your face in the course of an argument, your gifts laughed at, and your love abused. You conclude: "I'll never love again."

You think you've found a grand new friend and go everywhere with her, do everything with her, and suddenly she evaporates. You conclude, "People are horrible, you can't trust anybody."

You're enchanted with your new job, you put in unpaid overtime, you forget about coffee breaks, work right through lunch, and when you ask for an afternoon off, you're yelled at for being so demanding. You conclude, "I hate my job, they're terrible, they take advantage of me."

What do these three situations have in common? They all represent a painful example of "pearls before swine." You have a great deal to offer: "pearls" (your love, your talents, your qualities) in a friendship, a love relationship, or on the job, but if you offer these pearls blindly, without first looking to see if the person on the receiving end will treat your pearls with respect and appreciation, you're setting yourself up for pain. Too many people just aren't in a place where they can be automatically relied upon to appreciate you.

Take charge. Be responsible for who and how you give your pearls.

1. *Observe.* Before you go flying into a new relationship of any kind (friend, lover, work), observe how the person you're interested in treats other people, such as friends, employees, family, parking-lot attendants, waiters, his/her mother, and how he/she talks about other people. Does the person you're interested in treat other people with consideration? Does he/she pay attention when others speak? Does he/she behave with kindness or does he/she respond offhandedly, treating the other person more as a thing than as a human being? Does the person you're interested in talk about other people in positive ways, mentioning their qualities, their value, or does he/she put down other people, pointing out weaknesses and flaws?

Observe. You will be treated exactly like the way the person treats others. Don't think that "love" will make a difference. How we treat each other is the product of long-standing habits: These can be changed, but only over time and with persistent diligence. Love alone will not do it.

2. *Give a little at a time.* Don't give all of yourself (your time, your energy, your focus, your attention, your secrets, your talents, your love) all at once. Give a little of whatever, then stand back and watch what the person you're interested in does with it. If he/she treats your offering with respect and appreciation, terrific! Give a little more. Then stand back and watch.

Repeat this process, giving yourself the benefit of observation over time. That way, if he/she starts taking and taking without appreciation, or becomes abusing of your confidence, or comes up flaky, you'll know it way before you've given so much you end up feeling used and abused.

Protect your pearls! You are much too valuable to waste on unworthy people or jobs.

> *To change's one's life: Start immediately. Do it flamboyantly. No exceptions.*
>
> WILLIAM JAMES

Fairy Tales Do Come True

It is night. The princess flees the dragon, running, running into the woods. The handsome young prince charges up on his valiant steed, grabs the fearsome dragon by the throat, and shows the princess it was only a paper dragon, nothing to be feared at all. The princess sighs with relief. The prince looks soulfully into the princess's eyes and says, "I will take you wherever you want to go, beautiful one, you have but to say where." The princess looks away and says, "Where?"

> PRINCE: "Yes, tell me where you want to go."
>
> PRINCESS: "I don't know where."
>
> PRINCE: "Well, where were you running to?"
>
> PRINCESS: "I don't know, I was just running."
>
> PRINCE: "Forget it, lady, I'll just go find a princess who knows where she's going!"

Fairy tales aren't supposed to turn out this way. Yet this is all too often what happens when you stop being motivated by fear, pain, or anger. You know what you *don't* want running your life anymore, but you haven't chosen what you *do* want running your life.

You have taken a wonderful first step: You have decided, for example, that you no longer want to become successful to prove to your mother/wife/high-school friends that you are a worthwhile human being, or you have decided no longer to buy into your family's definition of life as "Life's a bitch and then you die." Now you need to go on to Step Two and decide what success means to you, and if life isn't a "bitch," then what is it?

If you don't define the goals and values you want for yourself, then you will find yourself drifting, eventually only to fall back into choices and behaviors motivated by that old trio—fear, pain, and anger. Attach yourself strongly to goals and values that pull you into the life you want.

Figure out, for example, what "success" means for you, in real practical terms that you can actually work toward. Perhaps "success" for you is having work that you enjoy that allows you time to be with your children. Fine. That goal gives you a direction to go in, it gives you a specific focus. Then go after it diligently. You are being motivated by a positive desire toward a defined goal. You may sometimes bump into your fears, pain, and anger, but that is all it will be—a manageable bump. Your focus and goal will keep you moving forward and on track.

Be picky about your goals and values. Goals are what you want, and values are what's important to you on the way there. Don't just adopt any old goal/value that somebody else has. Think about it, really figure out, "Is this something I truly want, that I truly believe in, or am I just following a party line?" If your goal/value ends up being the same as someone else's, that's fine, for now you will have consciously and deliberately chosen it as your own independently of the other person's.

You are a unique and valuable human being. You deserve to live life according to your dreams and your desires. Make the effort to figure out what those dreams and desires are, and then go for them with everything you've got.

*W*hen there is no vision, a people perish.

RALPH WALDO EMERSON

The Power of Words

He says "I love you," and you believe him. She says "I'll be faithful to you forever," and you believe her. Your employer says "Do good work and you'll get a promotion," and, of course, you believe him. Your coworker says "I never gossip about people," and you assume what you hear is truth.

When your boyfriend then calls you "stupid," "bitch," and "dumb," you are in shock; how could he say this if he loves you? When your girlfriend is caught kissing the guy next door, you're appalled. You wonder how much more good work you'll have to do (you've been on the job five years hearing only praise for your work) before that promised promotion happens, and when you find out that your supposedly nongossiping coworker has been repeating intimate details of your personal life to any and all who will listen, you are stunned. Why is this happening? What's going on?

You've been trapped by the power of words. It's as simple—and as potentially devastating—as that. We've all been conditioned to believe what we are told. Indeed, life as we know it couldn't go on without our ability to rely on what people tell us. So most of us go about our lives believing what we hear, trusting that it is "for real."

The problem lies not in our willingness to take what we are told as truth, but in our failure to consistently evaluate what we are *told* against what we *see*. People's actions are what will tell you whether a person's words are trustworthy or not. All of us want to believe that our mate loves us when he says "I love you," but "I love you" is a meaning-less phrase unless it is backed up with loving actions. There is nothing loving about being called demeaning names. There is nothing loving about being shoved, pushed, or hit. Your girlfriend's promise of fidelity is just fantasy on her part unless she indeed behaves in a way consis-tent with her words. If your employer promises promotions but never delivers (and your work truly is good), then your employer is just string-ing you along with empty words, never backing up those words with appropriate action.

So what to do? Never trust anything you hear? Become paranoid and stop believing everybody? No. Simply balance the extraordinary power of an individual's *words* with what you observe of the person's *actions*. Listen and watch, watch and listen. If your coworker says "I never gossip," trust her with some small piece of information that wouldn't damage you forever if heard by others. Then watch. Do your words come back to you out of another person's mouth? If so, you know that regardless of what your coworker says, she does gossip. Pay atten-tion. Does your coworker talk about other people's lives? Then regard-less of their "I never gossip," they do! When your employer fails to give you a promotion you feel you deserve, ask for specifics of what you need to do more. If, once you've done that, your employer still doesn't give you the promotion, then his words are just so much hot air and cannot be trusted.

If your boyfriend's actions are loving, then his "I love you" is sin-cere and can be trusted. Otherwise, his words may reflect his feelings, but he can't express those feelings in appropriate actions, and thus his words, as lovely as they are to the ear, are nothing more than empty promises.

Don't be fooled by words. Words do create expectations of behavior, expectations we then act upon and live by, which can be hurtful (sometimes deadly!) if those words are without the bedrock of matching behavior. Be willing to watch as well as listen, so that your hopes and dreams may be fulfilled and you may enjoy the happiness you deserve.

> *A thousand words will not leave so deep an impression as one deed.*
>
> HENRIK IBSEN

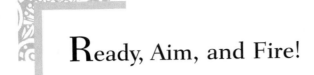

Ready, Aim, and Fire!

Congratulations! You've finally realized you're not life's doormat and you're ready to stand up for yourself. That's great! Only you find yourself caught in a dilemma: Either you state your needs in such a way that no one pays attention to you, or you come off like a raging bull and people pay attention to you all right, but it always ends up in fights or tears. Neither approach is satisfactory. What to do? Simple: Ready, aim, and fire. What does that mean?

1. *Be ready.* "Ready" means check your timing. There is a vast difference between standing up for what you want and need at the time you want it and standing up for what you want and need after you haven't gotten it. For example, you realize it bothers you that your colleague/spouse is always late. Paying attention to your timing means saying to your colleague/spouse before the next time she might be late: "It's very uncomfortable for me when you are late. I would appreciate it if you could make arrangements to be on time," rather than waiting until she is (once again) late and then, thoroughly disgusted and frustrated, having checked your watch every five minutes, blowing up at her. She may still choose to be late, but now she knows how you feel about it, and you have a basis for discussion.

2. *Aim.* Be clear about exactly what it is you want and need, and set up your request in such a way that you're likely to get it. Don't say, "You know, it's sort of a hassle, I mean it's not a big deal or anything, but it would be kinda nice if you could get to the meeting/restaurant/ball-

236

park on time." All the person is going to hear is "not a big deal"! Be clear. It is a big deal to you. It makes you uncomfortable, it interferes with your happiness. So say that: "It makes me uncomfortable . . ." and then set up your request with satisfaction in mind.

In this example you might ask what you can do to facilitate the other's timeliness, or explore with her why she tends to be late (maybe she isn't even aware of it), and so forth. To use a different example, if someone is rude to you, being clear may mean you let the person know the consequence of being rude to you: "I do not accept being talked to that way. If you continue, I will leave," and if he is still rude—leave! And so on.

To aim is to be clear about what you want and assume a problem-solving approach to getting it, rather than waffling around what you want and then punishing yourself or others when you don't get it.

3. *Fire.* Be direct and straightforward with both your body language and speech when you state your want. Look the other person in the eye, keep your body still (don't wiggle or squirm or clench your fists, it's distracting), and state your want in a firm, clear voice. Don't turn your request into a whine or a demand; be direct.

To summarize: Be assertive, not aggressive. State your wants and needs positively in a clear and direct manner; don't defend your needs tooth and claw after the fact (it's bloody and rarely works); don't sidle up to your needs in roundabout, diluted fashion and then be surprised that no one hears you. You deserve the best life has to offer, so—ready, aim, and fire!

> *There are two things to aim at in life: first, to get what you want; and after that, to enjoy it.*
>
> LOGAN PEARSALL SMITH

Redefining Failure

You go to work from 9:00 to 5:00, your job is OK, nothing special. You have an OK relationship, your kids are OK, your friends are OK, everything is OK in your life. And yet every once in a while you get that nagging thought, "Is this all there is?" And every once in a while when you're reading *People* magazine (at the dentist's, of course) you read about something someone has done—climbed a mountain, started an organization to help the homeless, written a bestseller, traveled the globe—and your first thought is, "Gosh, I wish I could do that," and your second thought is, "Nah, never happen." And you turn the page and read about someone else's dreams coming true, forgetting all about your own.

How sad. How common. And how totally avoidable. Huh? Yes—how totally avoidable. You see, the only difference between the people who are climbing mountains, and so on, and those who don't is that the ones climbing mountains don't let the fear of failure stop them. Everybody has that fear, but those who successfully pursue their dreams have found a way of dealing with the fear so it doesn't block them from achieving their goals.

How? Well, you can have fear of failure only if you believe in failure. If failure doesn't exist for you, you can't fear it. Ever watched a baby learning to walk? The idea of failure never enters into the equation. If it did, the baby would probably never make it. Every time she fell down, she would think she failed. So much for walking. Instead, what happens is the baby falls down hundreds of times, either laughs or cries depending on the nature of the fall, then picks herself up and starts over again.

There is no such thing as failure. There is only experiencing life and learning. If you adopt that point of view, everything becomes possible. If your dream has always been to play the guitar, do so for the joy of learning and experiencing what guitar playing is all about. You can't fail at learning and you can't fail at experiencing. Now, you may not learn to the extent that you had fantasized, and you may not experience earth-shattering, record-breaking success, but you will learn and experience guitar playing. The degree of your success will vary with the level of your personal potential and commitment.

If your dream is world peace, rather than cutting yourself off with "I could never do anything to help bring about world peace," go about it with the idea "I can learn about how to do that," and do it for the enjoyment of the experience. You can read up on what others have created as avenues to world peace. You can join organizations devoted to world peace and enjoy being with others of like mind. You can subscribe to journals dedicated to world peace. You can learn ways to be more peaceful in your own life. As you do so, you will inevitably contribute to bringing about world peace.

In other words, you cannot fail. However lofty the dream, you can achieve relative degrees of success. If you are coming from a place of learning/experiencing, you can also, at some point, decide you've learned/experienced as much as you'd like and move on to exploring something else—how much more self-esteeming than deciding you must have "failed," which puts a serious damper on your willingness to ever pursue another dream.

Taking the idea of failure out of your existence is wonderfully freeing. It allows you to focus on what is important, enjoying and experiencing life, rather than fearing failure, which leads to fearing life itself.

> *Few wishes come true by themselves.*
>
> JUNE SMITH

Putting an End to Self-Blame

Ever noticed how you talk to yourself when you've made a mistake or failed to do/be something the way you wanted to? The inner conversation between you and you often runs something like this: "I can't believe I said that to my boss. I am a complete moron. I have no brains, nothing. He's probably gonna fire me"; or, "Fifteen pounds! I can't believe I gained 15 pounds! I have no self-control, I'm a mess"; or, "She left me. I'm a zero, I'm not a real man. No one could possibly love me."

The situations may vary, but the inner talk is the same. You go from a very specific event (saying something dumb, gaining unwanted pounds, your lover leaving) to a demeaning conclusion about your general worth ("I'm a complete moron, I have no self-control, I'm a mess, I'm a zero, not a real man"), without even pausing to take a breath in between.

People often confuse blaming themselves with taking responsibility. Judging yourself an inept idiot for saying something dumb to your boss isn't taking responsibility, it's avoiding responsibility by taking on the role of victim: "Poor me, I'm so dumb, oh dear, I'll probably get fired;" "I gained 15 pounds, poor me, there's nothing I can do about it, I've got no self-control"; "I'm a zero, poor me, I'm hopeless, I'm totally unlovable."

In all of these the underlying theme is, "It's not my fault, it's just the way I am, and I can't help it." Judging yourself as being so bad the situation can't be remedied or improved is being a victim.

Taking responsibility is a different matter and would look something like this:

"I said something really dumb in front of my boss. What can I do to compensate for that? Can I do a really top-notch piece of work, put in extra hours, offer to help out with a special project? And what can I do to see to it I don't say something stupid in the future? Count to ten before I open my mouth, listen more, and talk less?"

"OK, so I gained 15 pounds. What can I do to lose them? Be more conscious of what's going on when I put food in my mouth, go to OA, take an aerobics class? And what can I do to see to it I don't gain them back? Learn more about my relationship to my body, consult a nutritionist?"

"All right, she left me. How can I approach this constructively? Can I seek to understand what each of us contributed to the relationship not working out, explore what I really want in a relationship anyway, see what parts of myself I want to grow and develop? What can I do to prevent a similar occurance in the future? Learn more about how relationships work, learn more about how I work, learn more about how others think and feel?"

These are ways of taking responsibility, of dealing positively with the mistakes and failures we all experience.

Avoiding responsibility does not get rid of the pain. Only as we take responsibility, seek to stretch and reach and grow, do we transform painful situations into vibrant, happy ones. You are a strong and worthy person. Don't deny your strength and worth, for in it there is great power.

A failure is a man who has blundered but is not able to cash in the experience.

ELBERT HUBBARD

The Power of Setting Limits

In the language of human relationships "setting limits" means letting people know what is acceptable to you and what is not. For example, if being hit by your spouse is not acceptable to you, then "setting limits" is saying, the first time your spouse hits you: "That is not acceptable to me. If you hit me again, I will leave," and the second time your spouse hits you, actually leaving. Setting limits is an expression of your human value, of your self-worth. By setting limits you say: "I'm a human being. I am valuable. I deserve to be treated well."

All that is well and good, but there is a second aspect to setting limits that is less recognized, yet just as important. Only by setting limits is it possible to give wholeheartedly and graciously. And the ability to give wholeheartedly and graciously is one of the basic components of true and lasting love.

How does this work? Well, let's say your mate wants to be affectionate and playful, but you've had a rough day at work/with the kids, and you desperately need some private time. If you're not good at setting limits, you'll probably try to force yourself to be affectionate and playful, which of course won't work because you're too stressed to relax, the end result being that you feel pressured, resentful at your mate for "demanding so much" of you, and further stressed. Your mate won't have much of a good time either, because she can feel your resentment whether or not you voice it.

If you know how to set limits, however, you can operate quite differently in a way guaranteed to further the love, not squash it. You can

243

say, for example: "Honey, I'd love to spend some fun time with you, but right now I'm very stressed from my day, and I need to unwind. How about if we do our separate thing for about an hour, and get together around 8:00?" You can then go off and do whatever you need to unwind, destress, and nurture yourself. Now when you get together with your mate, you really are ready, willing, and able to be there for her and to give graciously and wholeheartedly of your affection and playfulness.

Often when we love someone, we are tempted to do everything he/she wants when he/she wants it, because we're afraid the person will abandon us if we don't. But when you give to another at the price of hurting yourself, you do not give graciously, you give against a background of resentment that inevitably comes out in the form of martyrdom ("I do everything for you, can't you love me just a little?"), victim ("Nothing I ever do is good enough, nobody loves me"), or sour grapes ("Love—schmove. It's always the same: I give, they take"). And it is that underlying resentment that distorts love, damages it, and eventually drives your loved one away.

When we fail to set limits, giving becomes a problem. We either give too much or too little. Set limits: Take responsibility to ensure that your needs are met so that you then are free to give fully and joyously. Learning to set limits is a skill. As you practice it with your friends and loved ones, you will earn their respect and pave the way to truly loving relationships.

There is only one happiness in life, to love and be loved.

GEORGE SAND

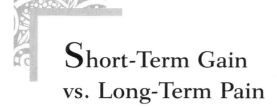

Short-Term Gain
vs. Long-Term Pain

You have so much going on, among the job, the kids, the dentist, the car, that you keep putting off balancing your checkbook and then WHAM! you bounce 13 checks in a row. . . .

You have a fling with a perfectly delightful man who told you up front that he had a problem with alcohol, but you ended up falling in love and now three years later you are in a committed relationship you don't know how to get out of with an alcoholic you resent. . . .

You took the job because the pay was decent and the boss was so eager to hire you, he seemed to think you were God walking and, boy, did that feel good, but now after only three months, the boss is after you all the time, you can't seem to do anything right, and you wonder, maybe you should have paid more attention to the extremely high turnover rate in this company before you took the job. . . .

The one thing these three apparently different situations have in common is a failure to look at long-term consequences, which too often lead to long-term pain. We are a fast-food, do-it-now, get-up-and-go society, and although that approach to life has propelled us into many successes, it has also cost us dearly in the long haul (for example, the sorry condition of our environment).

Balance your initiative and go-get-'em enthusiasms with careful thought as to where your decisions and choices are likely to lead you.

For example, if you think through just for a moment the consequences of not balancing your checkbook for a couple of months, you'll quickly realize that the likelihood of bouncing checks is very good. This will cost you check charges, inconvenience, and/or embarrassment. Make your decision regarding checkbook balancing taking long-term consequences into account.

If you meet someone you're attracted to and you think, "Oh, I'll just have a fling with him," think that through carefully. Can you just "have a fling"? Or do you tend to become emotionally involved with everyone you get sexually involved with? Look at the long-term consequences of your own character and tendencies. Factor that into your decision making. If the person lets you know up front he has a problem with alcohol, think about what that means for you long term. Don't stick your head in the sand, ostrich style, and pretend it won't matter or "love will conquer all." It does matter and love doesn't conquer all. Think about it, "Is this OK with me? How will this behavior impact my life? Is this something I can handle? Now, in two years, in five years, in twenty?" Looking honestly at the long-term consequences will greatly assist you in making the right decision for you.

If there's a high turnover rate in a company you're interested in working for, again, don't ignore that. Don't allow yourself to be charmed out of paying attention to such a valuable warning. Look into it; what does that say for you long term? Then make your decision based on your best assessment of those long-term consequences.

Don't let life just "happen" to you. Although there are no guarantees and life is assuredly full of surprises, by making well-thought-out decisions you'll greatly increase your opportunities for happiness.

Be realistic: plan for a miracle.

BHAGWAN SHREE RAJNEESH

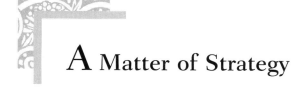

A Matter of Strategy

You've decided you want a new relationship—a new friend, a new lover, or you want to better a current relationship—with your spouse, or a stepchild, or a colleague at work, and so you make reservations at your favorite restaurant (even though you can't afford it right now), put on your favorite clothes, and are nice and cordial with the person, being as "interesting" as you know how, showing how well read or well informed you are, positively bursting with good intentions toward the person—and nothing happens: The friendship doesn't develop, the relationship doesn't get better . . . and off you trudge in the depths of despair: "Nobody loves me, I'll never have a friend, I must be a boring person, I can't even get my stepchild to talk to me," and so on.

What went wrong? In all likelihood, you're not an awful person; you just used a strategy that wasn't suited to your needs. Getting what you want and need is often a matter of picking the appropriate strategy.

For example, if you want a new friend, or a better relationship, and so on, first recognize that YOU are doing the wanting. Therefore YOU will have to do all the work. It's no different from getting carrots to grow. If you want carrots to grow, you have to till the soil, plant the carrot seeds, and nurture them carefully into existence; the carrot will not do that for you. So too, if you want the friend, the better relationship, be willing to do all the work to bring this thing you want into existence.

Second, get into the other person's world. One of our biggest mistakes is to assume because we want something a certain way, so does everybody else; nothing could be further from the truth. Everyone is unique, and your idea of a romantic evening or the ideal thing to do with a new friend may be the opposite of what that person enjoys. Observe the person, learn how he/she goes about his/her life, find out what pleases him/her. Remember, you're the one who wants the relationship; that means you have to find out what works for that person and start from his/her reality, not expect or demand that he/she fit into your reality.

Third, stop focusing on what that person can do for you ("He'll make me happy," "She'll put in a good word for me with the boss"), and focus on what you can do for the person. At this point the other person isn't motivated in the same way you are to create/better the relationship. The only way he/she is going to be motivated is if he/she sees what's in it for him/her (which sounds cold and calculating, but really isn't; it's the bottom line of how we operate). Find out what matters in this person's life, what makes him/her happy, and focus on how you can contribute to that happiness.

Last, be realistic in your expectations. As you observe the person you're interested in, ask yourself if indeed he/she is capable or available for the type of friendship/relationship you want. Depending on the circumstances of his/her life, people may or may not have the energy/willingness to be who and how you want them to be in your life.

You can't get what you want with the wrong strategy. Use the preceding points and discover how nice it is to have a strategy that works.

It's a funny thing about life; if you refuse to accept anything but the best, you very often get it.

W. SOMERSET MAUGHAM

On Being Supportive

You're not quite sure what to do. You're going for the first time to your new love's family get-together: Should you bring flowers? a cake? a bottle of wine? nothing? What would express that you're a kind and decent person or whatever it is that you want to express? You decide on a bottle of wine.

When you tell your friend, Sally, "I decided to take a bottle of wine," she says, "What a dumb idea, they're gonna think you're an alcoholic. Take a box of candy." You berate yourself for your dumb choice and take the candy. The family seems pleased. When after the get-together, you tell your Mom you took candy, she says, "I wouldn't have done that. You should have taken a nice bunch of flowers. But who listens to me, I'm just your mother." You then run the evening by a colleague who says, "Did you take them that nice bottle of Chablis you were thinking of?" and when you say "No," looks at you and says, "Oh, too bad." By now you feel lower than an earthworm. You are sure you took the wrong thing, you are too stupid for words, and the family only said they liked your gift to be "nice" (yuck). You want to crawl in a hole and die.

What happened here? You have just been criticized to death (literally). Rather than helping you make the decision that would be best for you, your friends and family were critical of what you chose/did.

We often mistake criticalness for supportiveness. If you think your friend is making an unwise decision, it may feel loving to tell your friend he's doing it wrong, and tell him how to go about it, but actually, it's very damaging. In the first place, everybody's different: What works for you may be lethal for your friend. In the second place, when you put down your friend's idea and substitute your own, you hurt your friend's feelings of competence and self-worth. Regardless of your good intent, your implied message is that he can't do it for himself. That isn't supportive.

Supportiveness is helping others understand and clarify their own thinking and decision making by discussing with them aspects of the situation they may not have considered, by suggesting choices they may not have thought of, and/or by pointing out where their thinking seems confusing or unclear. In the preceding example, Sally is concerned that taking a gift of wine connotes alcoholism. To be supportive, she could say, "Some people are really against drinking. Do you know how the family feels about that?" This response does not tell you what to do or put down your idea. It suggests an idea to take into consideration that might be useful in your decision making. If you replied, "Gee, that's right—and I think their Uncle is in AA," and your friend then said, "A lot of people like flowers. And I saw some great balloons in that new shop down the street," she would be suggesting alternatives, not dictating your choice.

We all need the loving input of our friends. Making that input supportive rather than critical is a loving and valuable act.

What the world really needs is more love and less paper work.

PEARL BAILEY

Taking vs. Receiving

There are so many things that we want in this life—faithful passionate rich lovers/spouses, high-status challenging jobs, well-behaved loving children who never talk back, toned energized bodies, and so on. And to get those things, we scheme and strategize and manipulate, and lo and behold, sometimes we actually get what we covet—only to lose it all too quickly. Why? Because you cannot keep what you take, you can only keep what you receive.

There is a vast difference between taking and receiving, and as long as your only way of getting the things you want is to take them, then you'll lose them somewhere down the road. Taking does not imply free giving. Taking (in the sense referred to here) comes out of what I call "see . . . want . . . grab." No matter how coyly or subtly you did the grabbing, the person you grabbed from is not likely to be happy about it.

Receiving, on the other hand, implies that the person freely gave you whatever it was and therefore is happy to have given it. People are much happier freely giving to others than they are having things grabbed from them.

For example, you want your spouse to be nice to you. So you moan and groan about what an awful day you had and top it off with, "See, you don't even care—you're not even listening," which guilts your spouse into forcing herself to pay attention to you/make nice/rub your back. So it works, short-term. But how long do you think "grabbing" niceness from your spouse by manipulating her with guilt is going to work? Your spouse is no dummy—eventually she'll figure it out and

251

either make herself scarce or just come out with "So you had a lousy day, so what!" Hardly what you want to hear.

But how do you receive niceness? Well, first off, you don't manipulate people into niceness. You have a choice of two good techniques.

1. *Give kindness.* Giving kindness sets up a dynamic whereby you will in turn receive kindness. For example, in coming home, you give your spouse the space/hugs/whatever it is that you know feels good to her; you are kind, knowing that your kindness will support her desire to be kind to you. You DO NOT do this manipulatively. You are just generally being kind knowing that kindness will be forthcoming for you—if not right then, soon. (This applies to normal, well-intentioned people. If your spouse is an unfeeling, uncaring person, this won't work and best you look at how you choose spouses.)

2. *Ask directly for what you want.* "Honey, I had a bad day and I'm really burnt out. Would you hold me for a while/rub my back/sit with me? It would feel very good to me."

In both 1 and 2, whatever kindness you get will have been given freely. And you can use those two techniques over and over and over, and people won't mind because they know they have a choice. You're no longer conning your spouse/child/employer into what you want, so although you cannot expect always to get your way, when you do get what you want, it will last.

How much more satisfying for all concerned to think in terms of receiving rather than taking!

> *Perfect kindness acts without thinking of kindness.*
>
> LAO-TSE

On Developing Trust

Trust is one of the most important elements of any successful relationship. It is also one of the most fragile and vulnerable. When you trust someone, you stand to lose a great deal should he betray your trust. You also cannot fully be yourself with someone and enjoy a deeply satisfying relationship unless you trust him.

Faced with such a paradox, we often feel stuck with an either/or choice: "Either I trust everybody, or I trust nobody," "Either I reveal myself totally to people, or I reveal nothing at all." Unfortunately, none of these choices are successful: You end up betrayed because in trusting everybody, someone is bound to betray you; in trusting nobody, you deprive yourself of the possibility of true relationship; in revealing all of yourself, someone is bound to take advantage of you somewhere along the line; in revealing nothing of yourself, you don't develop relationship.

The solution is not to throw up your hands in disgust, but rather to learn a two-step approach to developing trust safely.

1. *Take a calculated risk.* When you are first getting to know someone, take the risk of sharing with him some small, genuinely vulnerable portion of yourself, but be sure to calculate ahead of time that if he should betray your disclosure, the damage to you would be virtually nonexistent. For example, let the person know that you had a difficult time emotionally when your cat died and notice how he treats this disclosure. If he empathizes with you and seems sincere in appreciating what this was like for you, he's just taken one step in the right direction.

Now wait a while (a week, two weeks) and see if he does anything detrimental with that information: gossip about you, make derogatory remarks about people who grieve over their pets, "tease" you about it (it's rarely funny). If he doesn't do anything offensive, take the next calculated risk and disclose something else; wait and see what he does with it. Allowing your disclosure of self to happen in small bits and slowly over time is one of the surest ways to protect yourself from an untrustworthy individual.

2. *Observe whether or not the person's actions back up his words.* When somebody's actions are different from his words, believe his actions. If someone tells you that you are very important to him, but every time you have an appointment with him, he is late—then regardless of his "reasons," you aren't that important to him! And much as that may sting in the first few weeks of getting to know someone, it is far better to evaluate correctly where you stand with someone in the first few weeks of getting to know each other than to get into a long-term relationship (love/work/friendship) where you finally figure out, after having been mistreated 100 times, that maybe you don't really matter to this person.

Listen to what people say, and then watch what they do—trustworthy people back up their words with action 95 percent of the time (nobody's perfect).

Learn to develop trust safely, and you'll enjoy the wonderful relationships you deserve.

> $\mathcal{D}$o not weep; do not wax indignant. *Understand.*
>
> BARUCH SPINOZA

On Getting Unstuck

Change is hard for all of us, especially personal change. If you have a bad habit or are in a rotten relationship or can't stand your job, often it seems as if change is virtually impossible. And so you stay stuck, moaning and groaning, never enjoying your life the way it was meant to be enjoyed. A lot of what "stuckness" is about, however, is just misusing the past, present, and future as points of reference.

1. *Getting stuck in the past.* You look to the past as a reference for "Well that's how things always work out," completely ignoring the fact the future is a giant unknown. To cite but a couple of the amazing events of the 1990s: Who ever thought the Berlin Wall would come down? If we looked only to the past as a reference, that was impossible. Post-menopausal women are having babies; in the past, that was impossible.

The past has great usefulness as an explainer of how you got where you are. Your parents, for example, were cold and unloving; you therefore had no role model for a truly loving relationship, and so you unconsciously picked a mate who fit right in with what was familiar to you—cold and unloving. But that's the extent of the usefulness of the past. Once you've acquired an understanding, you're ready to choose what you want to have happen in the unknown of the future.

2. *Getting stuck in the future.* That's another place people get stuck . . . the unknown of the future. You get stuck on the fear of the unknown and ignore the marvelous opportunity the unknown gives you to create virtually anything. There are no limits to what you can conceive in the

future, since the future is a wide-open space. The future is the perfect place in which to project your dreams and aspirations. You may not make it all happen, but the future gives you a point of reference to work toward.

3. *Getting stuck in the present.* The present is for doing and being. The present is a great place to be fully conscious of what you are doing or how you are being. Once you have gained an understanding of how things got where they are by referring to the past, the present is how you get step by step to your dreams in the future. People get stuck in the present by ignoring the reality of what they are doing and being and by operating on automatic pilot. Automatic pilot leads nowhere.

Getting unstuck: So how do you use the past, present, and future to facilitate change, to help you get where you want to go? Look to the past for understanding, figure out why things are the way they are for you. Then make choices. Ask yourself, "Is this how I want my life to look?" Determine what your dreams and desires are and then project those dreams and desires as already fulfilled in the future. Make clear images for yourself of what you want to have happen, and then let yourself be pulled by those images, so now you are not being pushed by a past that no longer exists, but rather are being motivated by the future you intend to create. Then use the present to do and be in ways that will allow that future to manifest.

Life can be such a glorious adventure. You don't have to stay stuck in unhappiness. Learn from your past, set your sights on a wondrous future, and enjoy making it happen in your here and now!

Our life is at all times and before anything else the consciousness of what we can do.

JOSE ORTEGA Y GASSET

The Power of "Wei Chi"

The love of your life deserts you for another man; the promotion you've been doing umpteen hours of (unpaid) overtime to land goes to the assistant you trained; you find out the funny skin thing you have is the first symptom of melonoma; you get laid off the job of your dreams because of the recession; you get rear-ended on the freeway by an uninsured motorist (yes, they still exist) in your pride-and-joy 1975 classic . . . These are all crises, and all of us, at one time or another of our lives, will have to face a crisis and deal with them.

But that's where the problem is. All too often, people don't face the crisis, and so you deal with it in a less than satisfactory manner and end up not feeling good about yourself, others, or about life in general.

Well, if you're not facing the crisis, what are you doing? Running away. Running away from the crisis in one of two ways: either by dumping the whole mess onto "the world" or onto "them" ("The economy is shot, that's why I got the ax," "He was nothing but a jerk"); or by dumping on yourself, getting self-destructive (alcohol, drugs, bingeing) or depressed ("I'm just a no-good/unsexy/stupid person, I'll never have a great relationship/job/car ever.")

Running away misses the point entirely. The Chinese put it well: The Chinese word for crisis is composed of two characters—"wei," meaning "danger," and "chi," meaning "opportunity." What an empowering definition of crisis! Once you know that both danger and opportunity are inherent to any crisis, you don't have to settle for running away by dumping your crisis onto others or yourself; you can face it squarely and look for the danger and the opportunity.

For example, the love of your life drops you mercilessly. The danger is that because you feel terribly hurt and angry, you may do self- or other-directed destructive things and come to negative conclusions about life. Knowing this is a danger, you can guard against it by seeking the support and help of your friends, family, a support group, a therapist, books, prayer; the opportunity may be to learn how to deliberately create successful relationships, or to experience the joy of being independent, or any number of things.

Or, say you find out you have cancer. The danger is to wallow in self-pity and despair; the opportunity is to investigate all the possibilities for a cure, or reassess your priorities and structure your life differently so that you do more of what you really enjoy, or be an example to others in a similar situation by your courage and dedication. The list goes on. Notice that the list of possible opportunities is always at least as long as the list of dangers.

Once you view crises in terms of danger and opportunity, you can deal with them in a healthy, productive way. Facing and dealing positively with a crisis becomes just another part of living life—a part that requires effort, no doubt, but a part that can help you grow, not doom you to despair.

Man never made any material as resilient as the human spirit.

BERN WILLIAMS